A PRIMER IN LONGITUDINAL DATA ANALYSIS

T 1

2

3

4

A PRIMER IN LONGITUDINAL DATA ANALYSIS

TOON TARIS

SAGE Publications

London • Thousand Oaks • New Delhi

SAGE Publications Ltd
6 Bonhill Street
London EC2A 4PU

SAGE Publications Inc.
2455 Teller Road
Thousand Oaks, California 91320

SAGE Publications India Pvt Ltd
32, M-Block Market
Greater Kailash – I
New Delhi 110 048

British Library Cataloguing in Publication data

A catalogue record for this book is available
from the British Library

ISBN 0 7619 6026 0 (hb)
ISBN 0 7619 6027 9 (pb)

Library of Congress catalog card number 00 131484

Typeset by Mayhew Typesetting, Rhayader, Powys
Printed in Great Britain by Redwood Books,
Trowbridge, Wiltshire

Contents

Preface

longitudinal – good for non-experimental
– issues of causality
– issues of change

The last three decades of the 20th century have witnessed a growing interest in the collection and analysis of longitudinal data – that is, data describing the course of events during a particular time period, rather than at a single moment in time. Today, longitudinal data are considered indispensable for examining issues of causality and change in non-experimental survey research. This is also reflected in the increasing numbers of publications reporting the results of longitudinal data analyses. Whereas in 1970 only about 0.6 per cent of the publications abstracted in the Psyclit database (a database containing information about more than 1,500,000 articles that have appeared since 1889 in the leading psychology journals) included the term 'longitudinal', the equivalent proportion for the articles published in 1997 was 3.8 per cent. For the publications in the Sociofile (consisting of abstracts of articles that appeared in the prominent sociology journals) and Medline (medicine) databases, the corresponding figures were 0.2 (1.7) per cent for 1970, and 6.6 (10.4) per cent for 1997, respectively. Clearly, nowadays researchers must at least have a working knowledge of the basics of longitudinal research – either because they themselves are (planning to get) involved in longitudinal research, or because they must judge the work of others.

This book is intended for students and researchers who want to learn how to collect and analyze longitudinal data. It may also be used as a handbook and a reference guide for users in practical research. I have especially attempted to illustrate the entire research path required in conducting longitudinal research: (1) the design of the study; (2) the collection of longitudinal data; (3) the application of various statistical techniques to longitudinal data; and (4) the interpretation of the results. As such, this text may be considered a sort of 'survival kit', presenting the basics of the whole process of conducting longitudinal research. It was written in an attempt to provide the audiences mentioned above with a text that addresses the main issues and problems in longitudinal data collection and analysis in an accessible, yet thorough fashion. Given the intended audience – relative novices to longitudinal research, who are (or may become) involved in it, but who are not interested in statistical methods as such – the level of mathematical knowledge that is required is kept to a minimum. A working knowledge of correlational analysis, regression analysis and analysis of variance at the level of a first-year course in statistics will suffice. Further, each chapter

4 steps
① design
② data collection
③ statistical analyses
④ results interpretation

contains a section listing more specialized texts that interested readers may want to consult.

Chapter 1 provides a general introduction to the topic of longitudinal research, including a discussion of several approaches to collecting longitudinal data. Chapter 2 deals with the issue of missing data, while Chapter 3 addresses various forms of across-time change that may occur (paying special attention to the invariance of factor structures). Chapters 4 through 7 deal with a variety of special statistical techniques that may be used to analyze longitudinal data. Chapters 4 and 5 focus on techniques appropriate for analyzing panel data – that is, data collected at discrete points in time. These chapters assume that no information is available concerning the period between these time points. Chapter 4 is concerned with classical problems in the analysis of panel data, such as the use of change scores, regression to the mean, and cross-lagged panel analysis, in the context of regression models. Chapter 5 deals with repeated-measures analysis of variance, paying special attention to the problems that occur when this technique is applied to longitudinal non-experimental survey data.

Chapters 6 and 7 present methods for the analysis of event history-data, that is, data consisting of sequences of qualitative states (such as 'employed', 'married', and 'attending school'), the timing of transitions from one state to another, and the scores on other variables. Thus, whereas Chapters 4 and 5 present techniques suitable for the analysis of data collected at discrete time intervals, the techniques presented in Chapters 6 and 7 explicitly presume that information about the timing of transitions from one state to another is available – even if these transitions occurred between the waves of a study. Chapter 6 presents a discussion of various modes of continuous-time and discrete-time survival analysis, focusing on the prediction of particular transitions. In contrast, Chapter 7 is concerned with the analysis of event histories taken as wholes. This chapter presents methods to characterize the across-time development of event histories, as well as approaches to create classifications of similar event histories.

This book was largely written during the period when I was affiliated with the Department of Social Psychology of the Free University Amsterdam. However, it was completed at the Department of Social and Organizational Psychology of Utrecht University, The Netherlands. I owe much to opportunities for exchange of views with students and with senior colleagues, notably, in the latter case, as a member of a multidisciplinary research group on the socialization process of young adults. Pieter Drenth, Hans van der Zouwen, and Jacques Hagenaars head the long list of others from whom I have learned. The material presented in Chapter 7 is partly drawn from three papers that were written in collaboration with some of my colleagues. As such, this chapter reflects their ideas as much as mine, and they deserve it to be mentioned here. The first part of Chapter 7 is based on a paper written in collaboration with Jan Feij. The part on correspondence analysis of event

histories is based on a paper which was co-authored by Peter van der
Heijden. The final part of Chapter 7 (concerning order-based modes of
analysis) is based on a paper written with Wil Dijkstra, who also developed
the program that was used for analyzing the sequences. Of course, I alone
bear the responsibility for any errors in this chapter. Finally, this book is
dedicated to Inge, Marit, Kiki and Crispijn – the women and the man in my
life. My thanks to one and all.

Hilversum/Utrecht, October 1999
Toon Taris

chapters

1. Intro

2. Missing data

3. Change across time

4.) Analyzing   – change scores, regression to
5.) Panel data   the mean
                    – repeated measures

6. Survival analysis

7. Event history analysis

panel – data collected at discrete
        points in time

longitudinal — subjects over time
(series of time points)

cross-sectional — subjects at one time point

1   Longitudinal Data and Longitudinal Designs

This chapter deals with some of the issues and complexities involved in the collection of longitudinal data. It aims to provide guidance, ideas, and perhaps some sense of confidence to investigators who expect a longitudinal design to help them in obtaining valid answers to their research questions, but are as yet uncertain about the best design for such a study. In this chapter I first distinguish between longitudinal research *designs* and longitudinal *data*, showing that the last does not necessary imply the first, and vice versa. After discussing some of the advantages of longitudinal data, seven basic designs for collecting such data are addressed. Finally, I provide a short checklist of the issues to be considered before undertaking a longitudinal study.

Longitudinal data versus longitudinal designs

Basically, longitudinal data present information about what happened to a set of research units (such as people, business firms, nations, cars, etc.) during a series of time points (for simplicity, I will refer to human subjects throughout the remainder of this text). In contrast, cross-sectional data refer to the situation at one particular point in time. Longitudinal data are usually (but not exclusively) collected using a longitudinal research design. The participants in a typical longitudinal study are asked to provide information about their behavior and attitudes regarding the issues of interest at a number of separate occasions in time (also called the 'phases' or 'waves' of the study). The number of occasions is often quite small – longitudinal studies in the behavioral and social sciences usually involve just two or three waves. The amount of time between the waves can be anything from several weeks (or even days, minutes, or seconds, depending on the aim of a study) to more than several decades. Finally, the number of participants in the study is usually fairly large (say, 200 participants or over; sometimes even tens of thousands).

Although longitudinal research designs can take on very different shapes, they share the feature that the data describe what happened to the research units during a series of time points. That is, data are collected for the same

longitudinal -
intra - individual
comparisons

set of research units for (but not necessarily *at*) two or more occasions, in principle allowing for intra-individual comparison across time. Note that the research units may or may not correspond with the sampling units. For example, in a two-wave longitudinal study on the quality of the care provided by a children's day care center (the research unit), a different sample of parents (the sampling units) may be interviewed at each occasion. The aggregate of the parents' judgements at each time point will allow for conclusions about changes in the quality of the care provided by the center, even if no single parent has been interviewed twice.

As another example, take the *consumer panel* that is frequently used in marketing research. The participants in such panels provide the researchers on a regular basis with information about their level of consumption of particular brands or products. These levels are then monitored in time. However, the consecutive measurements are usually not matched at the micro-level of households (Van de Pol, 1989). Although this example presents a longitudinal study at the level of the research units (the brands under examination, the levels of consumption of these being followed across time), a series of cross-sectional studies would have given us the same information.

Thus, there is not necessarily a one-to-one correspondence between the design of a study and the type of data collected. The data obtained using a longitudinal research design (involving multiple interviews with the same participants) may be analyzed in such a way that no intra-individual comparisons are made; it may even be pointless to attempt to do so (as in the consumer panel). Conversely, longitudinal data may be collected in a single-wave study, by asking questions about what happened in the past (so-called retrospective questions, see below for a discussion). Although such data are collected at the same occasion, they may cover an extended period of time. As Campbell (1988: 47) argued, 'To define "longitudinal" and "repeated measures" synonymously is to confuse the design of a particular study with the form of the data one wishes to obtain'.

Covariation and causation

A distinction can be made between studies that are mainly of a descriptive nature, and studies that more or less explicitly aim to explain the occurrence of a particular phenomenon (Baltes and Nesselroade, 1979). In descriptive studies, the association (or covariation) between particular characteristics of the persons under study is described. Thus, researchers are satisfied with describing how the values of one variable are associated with the values of other variables. Conclusions in this type of research typically take the form of 'if X is the case, Y is usually the case as well', and 'members of group A have on average more of property X than members

$y \leftrightarrow x$ *description (association, covariation)*
$y \leftarrow x$ *causal (prediction)*

of group B'. Such statements simply describe what is the case; in a longitudinal context they would tell you what has happened to whom. The strength of the association between variables X and Y can be expressed through association measures such as the correlation coefficient (if both variables are measured on at least ordinal level) or the chi-square value (if both variables are measured qualitatively).

It is often unsatisfactory to observe a particular association without being able to say why this particular association exists. Further, from a practical point of view it is much more helpful to know that phenomenon Y is affected by X, rather than to know that X and Y tend to coincide. Therefore, it is not surprising that much research aims to explain the occurrence of events, to understand why particular events happen, and to make predictions when the situation changes (Marini and Singer, 1988). Stated differently, much research describes the association between pairs of variables in causal terms. It is generally accepted that at least the following three criteria must have been satisfied before a particular association between two variables can be interpreted in causal terms (Blalock, 1964; Menard, 1991).

1 *Covariation.* There must be a statistically significant association between the two variables of interest. It makes little sense to speak of a 'causal' relationship if there is no relationship at all.

2 *Non-spuriousness.* The association between the two variables must not be due to the effects of other variables. In experimental contexts this is ascertained by random allocation of participants to conditions. If successful, this results in a situation in which there are no pre-treatment differences between the experimental group and the control group, thus ruling out alternative explanations for a post-treatment difference. In non-experimental contexts, the association between two phenomena must hold up, even when other (sets of) variables are controlled. For example, a statistically significant relationship between the number of rooms in one's house and the price of the car that one drives will probably fully be accounted for by one's income. A statistical association between two variables that disappears after controlling a third variable is called 'spurious'.

3 *Temporal order of events.* Thirdly, the 'causal' variable must precede the 'effect' variable in time. That is, a change in the causal variable must not occur after a corresponding change in the effect variable (but see below).

A fourth criterion is not usually mentioned, perhaps because it is so obvious. Causal inferences cannot directly be made from empirical designs, irrespective of the research design that has been used to collect the data or the statistical techniques used to analyze the data. In non-experimental research, causal statements are based primarily on substantive hypotheses

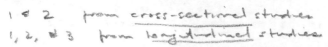

which the researcher develops about the world. Causal inference is theoretically driven; causal statements need a theoretical argument specifying how the variables affect each other in a particular setting across time (Blossfeld and Röhwer, 1997; Freeman, 1991). Thus, causal processes cannot be demonstrated directly from the data; the data can only present relevant empirical evidence serving as a link in a chain of reasoning about causal mechanisms.

The first two criteria (there is a statistically significant association between two variables, that is not accounted for by other variables) can in principle be tested using data from cross-sectional studies. Evidence relevant to the third criterion (cause precedes effect) can usually only be obtained using longitudinal data. Thus, one great advantage of longitudinal data over cross-sectional data would seem that the first provides information relevant to the temporal order of the designated 'causal' and 'effect' variables. Indeed, some authors (e.g., Baumrind, 1983) maintain that causal sequences cannot usually be established unambiguously without incorporating across-time measurement. However, there has been some debate whether the causal order of events is accurately reflected in their temporal order (Griffin, 1992): Is it *really* informative to know the order in which events occurred?

According to Marini and Singer (1988), causal priority may be established in the mind in a way that is not reflected in the temporal sequence of behavior. Willekens (1991) argued that present behavior may be determined by future events (or the anticipation of such events), rather than by these events themselves. For example, one common finding is that women tend to quit their job after the birth of their first child. These two events (leaving the labor market and having a baby) tend to coincide, with empirically occurring patterns in which childbirth both precedes and follows leaving the job. The first sequence would suggest that having a baby 'produces' a change of labor market status, whereas the second would imply that leaving the labor market leads to childbirth. However, it would seem that both events are the result of anticipations and decisions taken long before the occurrence of either. If this is correct, the temporal order of these events may not say much about their causal relation (Campbell, 1988).

The take-home message is that, although longitudinal data do provide information on the temporal order of events, it still may or may not be the case that there is a causal connection between these events. We still need to develop a more or less explicit theory that spells out the causal processes that produce empirically occurring patterns of events. A cautious investigator will consider these processes before the study is actually carried out – that is, in the design phase: a priori consideration of the possible relations among the study variables may lead them to conclude that other variables must be measured as well.

⊘ with longitudinal, we still may not have causality

Designs for collecting longitudinal data

[handwritten: 3 design issues (occasions of meas.) ① number of waves ② variables ③ sample]

Any study can only be as good as its design. This obvious (albeit often neglected) point applies strongly to longitudinal research, as the design of a longitudinal study must usually be fixed long before the last wave of this study has been conducted. Errors in the design phase may be costly and difficult (if not impossible) to correct – it is awkward to find out afterwards that it would have been very convenient had variable X been measured at the first wave of the study, rather than only at its final wave.

At a more basic level, investigators must decide in advance about the number of waves of their study; whether it is really necessary to measure the variables of interest at different times for the same set of sampling units; and about the number of sampling units for which data should be collected (taking into account that sampling units have the sad tendency to drop out of the study, see Chapter 2). Below I describe seven basic design strategies, all of which are frequently employed in practice (Kessler and Greenberg, 1981; Menard, 1991). Some of these are truly longitudinal, in that they involve multiple measurements from the same set of sampling units; others are not usually thought of as 'longitudinal' designs.

The simultaneous cross-sectional study

[handwritten: Jeff's previous research]

In this type of research, a cross-sectional study involving several distinct age groups is conducted. Each age sample is observed regarding the variables of interest. Although this design does not result in data describing change across time (it is therefore not a truly longitudinal design), it does yield data relevant to describing change across age groups. As such, it may be used to obtain understanding of development or growth across time. Any cross-sectional study in which participant age is measured might be considered an example of this design. However, in a simultaneous cross-sectional study, respondent age is the *key* variable, whereas in most 'standard' cross-sectional designs age is just another variable to be controlled.

There are many threats to the validity of inferences based on this type of study. For example, different age groups have usually experienced different historical circumstances, and these may also result in differences among the age groups (this point is elaborated below, in the discussion of the cohort study). Further, in this design, age effects are confounded with developmental effects, because the two concepts are measured with the same variable.

The trend study

In a trend study (which is sometimes also referred to as a 'repeated cross-sectional study'), two or more cross-sectional studies are conducted at two or more occasions. The participants in the cross-sectional studies are comparable in terms of their age. Usually a different sample is drawn from the population of interest for each cross-sectional study. In order to ensure the comparability of the measurements of the concept of interest across time, the same questionnaires must be used in all cross-sectional surveys (see also Chapter 3). This type of design is suitable to provide answers to questions like 'are adolescents becoming more sexually permissive?', or 'how does voters' support for right-wing parties vary across time?'.

In a typical trend study, researchers are not interested in examining change at the individual level (it is impossible to know what happened to whom, assuming that the study did not include retrospective questions). The trend study design is therefore not suited to resolve issues of causal order or to study developmental patterns. Its principal advantage to a true cross-sectional design is that it allows for the detection of change at the *aggregate* level. Thus, the trend study is a typical instance of a design that is cross-sectional at the level of the sampling units, but longitudinal at the level of the research units.

③ Time series analysis

In time series analysis, repeated measurements are taken from the same set of participants. The measurements are not necessarily equally spaced in time. In comparison to the two preceding designs, the time series design allows for the assessment of intra-individual change, because the same participants are observed across time. If different age groups are involved in the study, differences between groups with respect to intra-individual development may be examined. The time series design is very general and flexible. The intervention study and the panel study (see below) may be considered as variations on the time series design, involving many participants, many variables, and a limited number of measurements. In contrast, the term 'time series analysis' is usually reserved for studies in which a very limited number of subjects is followed through time at a large number of occasions and for a small number of variables.

④ The intervention study

The classic example of an intervention study is the pretest–posttest control group design (Campbell and Stanley, 1963). In this design, there is an experimental and a control group. The effects of a particular intervention (also termed *treatment* or *manipulation*) are studied by comparing the pretest and posttest scores of the experimental and the control group. In experimental (laboratory) studies, random assignment of participants to the control and experimental groups ensures that there are no important differences between the groups as regards possible confounding variables. This means that this design is a powerful means of assessing causal relations; if the experimental and the control group were comparable in terms of their pretest scores and participants were randomly assigned to these groups, a difference between the groups on the posttest measurement must be attributed to the experimental manipulation.

In survey research, however, random assignment of participants to experimental and control groups is usually unethical, impractical, or impossible, whereas the occurrence of the manipulation is often beyond the investigator's control (compare Chapter 5). Conscience will not let experimenters randomly assign children to experimental and control groups in order to examine the effects of growing up in a one-parent family on, say, substance abuse. In practice, some of the participants experience a particular event during the observed interval (such as the death of their spouse, the separation of their parents, etc.), whereas others do not. It is likely that the 'experimental' group (comprising the participants who experienced the event of interest) differed initially from the 'control' group. For example, if the event of interest is the death of a spouse, it would seem likely that the experimental group is on average quite a bit older than the control group. Insofar as such differences are relevant to the research question, they must be statistically controlled in order to ensure valid inferences. This 'nonequivalent control group design' (Cook and Campbell, 1979) is currently very popular in quasi-experimentation and survey research.

The panel study

In the panel study, a particular set of participants is repeatedly interviewed using the same questionnaires. The term 'panel study' was coined by the famous sociologist Paul H. Lazarsfeld when he reflected on the presumed effect of radio advertising on product sales. Traditionally, hearing the radio advertisement was assumed to increase the likelihood that the listeners would buy the corresponding product. Lazarsfeld considered the reverse relationship (people who have purchased the product might notice the advertisement, whereas others would not) plausible as well, casting doubts on the causal direction of this relationship. Lazarsfeld proposed that repeatedly interviewing the same set of people (the 'panel') might clarify this issue (Lazarsfeld and Fiske, 1938). However, long before Lazarsfeld, researchers routinely conducted studies involving repeated measurements (for example, in studies on childhood development: Nesselroade and Baltes, 1979; Sontag, 1971). Menard (1991) notes that national censuses have been taken at periodic intervals for more than three hundred years. According to Van de Pol (1989), the earliest example of a panel study in the sense of multiple measurements taken from the same set of participants is Engel's (1857) budget survey, examining how the amount of money spent on food changes as a function of income.

There are at least two reasons for the current popularity of the panel study. The first is that in a panel study information can be collected about change on the micro (sampling units) level. The amount of change can be related to other variables in the study using appropriate statistical models (see Chapters 4–7). Thus, a panel design enables researchers to observe relationships across time, rather than relationships at one point in time only. The second reason concerns the costs of data collection. A five-wave panel study may actually be cheaper to conduct than five separate cross-sectional studies. The costs of keeping a sample up to date (see Chapter 2) may well be lower than the costs of drawing a new random sample for each successive cross-sectional study. The consumer panel discussed earlier in this chapter consitutes an example of this approach.

The retrospective study

One distinct disadvantage of prospective longitudinal studies (such as the panel study or the intervention study) is that across-time analyses can only be conducted after at least two waves of data collection have been completed. As there may be several years between these waves, prospective longitudinal studies appeal strongly to one's patience. Further, a longitudinal study is much more expensive than a cross-sectional study (Powers et al., 1978). Think of how easy our life would be if we could ask our participants to tell us *now* what they did and felt *in the past*!

This idea has generated a considerable body of research, examining the reliability and accuracy of recall data – that is, data collected through asking questions about the past ('retrospective questions'). Inclusion of retrospective questions in a questionnaire would seem a quick and easy way to collect information about what happened to the participants in the past. Unfortunately, the quality of the answers given to such questions seems rather bad. On the basis of a literature review, Bernard et al. (1984) estimated that about half of the responses given on retrospective questions are probably in some way incorrect. Clearly, there is cause for concern as regards the quality of recall data.

Schwarz (1990, 1996) distinguishes among five distinct tasks that participants must accomplish when they provide an answer to a question about past behaviors. First, they must interpret the question to understand what they are supposed to report. Second, they have to recall relevant instances of this behavior from memory. Third, they must determine whether the recalled instances fall within or outside the intended reference period (the 'dating' of particular events). Fourth, they may rely on their general knowledge or other salient information to infer an answer. Finally, they have to communicate the result of their efforts to the interviewer – this may involve the 'editing' of the judgement to fit the response alternatives provided or the situation, due to influences of social desirability and situational adequacy.

There are two types of response errors, namely memory errors and reporting errors (Van der Vaart, 1996). *Reporting errors* may occur when communicating a response to the outside world. For example, Schwarz (1990) reported that black respondents were less likely to express explicit distrust of whites when the interviewer was white; conversely, white respondents muted negative sentiments about blacks when the interviewer was black. It is likely that these answers reflected a tendency to provide socially desirable answers. Reporting errors are not confined to retrospective questions, and may occur in almost any type of research.

Memory errors occur during the retrieval of information from memory. Ideally, researchers would like the participants in their study to use a 'recall and count' model when they answer a question about the frequency of their past behaviors. The respondents are expected to scan the intended period, retrieve all relevant instances, and count them in order to provide an accurate estimate of the frequency of that behavior (Schwarz, 1990). Unfortunately, people do not have that type of detailed representations of the individual instances of particular behaviors stored in memory. Rather, their answers are based on some fragmented recall and the application of inference rules to compute a frequency estimate (see Schwarz and Sudman, 1994, for extensive reviews). In the worst case, information collected by means of retrospective questions may present a severely distorted and inaccurate picture of past behaviors – little more than random error.

It is convenient to distinguish between two types of memory errors that may occur when inquiring into the past. First, respondents may have omitted relevant pieces of information. Respondents may be unable to recall a particular item in memory, or they may be unable to distinguish one item from another in memory (Linton, 1982). In effect, relevant instances of behaviors may be partly or completely forgotten. One strategy to help respondents recall relevant instances of past behaviors is by providing appropriate *recall cues*, usually instances of the class of behaviors that the researcher wants the respondent to recall. For example, Schwarz (1990) found that when respondents were asked how often they had eaten dinner in a regular or fast-food restaurant, they reported on average 20.5 instances for a three-month period. This increased to 26.0 instances when Schwarz specifically enquired after the number of times the respondents had had dinner in Chinese, Greek, Italian, Mexican, American, and fast-food restaurants, respectively. Thus, breaking down the question in a series of separate questions about eating in different types of restaurants seems to have been successful in helping the respondents recall relevant instances of these events. The difficulty with this approach is that respondents are likely

errors
① reporting (social desirability)
② memory

to omit instances that do not match the specific cues if these are not mentioned, resulting in underreports if the list is not exhaustive.

Second, retrospectively collected data may be distorted. Respondents tend to misestimate dates of events, or situate events in the wrong time period (Schwarz, 1990). People tend to assume that distant events happened more recently than they actually did, whereas the reverse applies to recent events ('forward' and 'backward telescoping', respectively). Reference periods that are defined in terms of weeks or months have been found to be highly susceptible to misinterpretations. A phrase like 'during the last year' may be construed as referring to the last calendar year, to the last twelve months, and/or as in or excluding the current month. 'Anchoring' the reference period with specific dates is not very helpful either, as respondents will usually be unable to relate a particular date to the events of interest. One potentially effective strategy is to anchor the reference period with salient personal or public events, so-called 'landmark events'. For example, Loftus and Marburger (1983) used the eruption of a volcano (Mount St Helens, which erupted six months before they conducted their study) to anchor the reference period, asking their respondents whether they had been victims of crime since this eruption. Their reports were compared with those of respondents who were asked whether they had been victims of crime in the last six months. On average, the 'eruption' question resulted in lower victimization reports, and validation information revealed that this question resulted in more accurately dated events. Moreover, they showed that more mundane landmarks such as 'Christmas' or 'New Year's Eve' increased recall accuracy as well.

Freedman et al.'s (1988) *life history calendar* (LHC) also uses landmarks to improve recall accuracy. The LHC is applied during interviews to administer the answers of respondents about multiple events and states that occurred during a certain period of time. It consists of a large two-dimensional grid in which one dimension represents the time units, while the other dimension specifies the events to be recorded. The respondents may see the LHC during the interview, but it is usually completed by the interviewer. One typical strategy to complete the LHC is to let the respondents mention events of which they know the dates and which are particularly salient to them (such as date of marriage, childbirth, etc.). These 'personal landmarks' may be used to anchor the reference period. Naturally, the grid may include 'public' landmarks as well – it would be folly not to take advantage of a recent eruption of your local volcano! Only after the reference period has been anchored sufficiently well does the interviewer inquire about the events of interest.

The major advantage of a LHC is that it may improve data quality by helping the respondent in relating the timing of several kinds of events to each other. Different activities are placed within the same time frame, and one event may prompt the recall of another. Major drawbacks of this procedure are that completing the grid tends to take much time, and that it requires considerably more intensive interviewer training. In the Freedman et al. (1988) case, the amount of time spent on interviewer training was tripled. More importantly, the effectiveness of this procedure has as yet not unequivocally been established: does the LHC really improve recall accuracy, and – if so – under which circumstances? The results of the rather limited amount of research on this issue are quite mixed. Below we briefly review the results of three more or less typical studies.

- Van der Vaart (1996) conducted a longitudinal field study among 1259 Dutch youth. At the first wave of the study the participants provided information about their marital status, employment record and the like. They were contacted again four years later. One half of the participants recalled information regarding the variables mentioned above with the help of a LHC, while the other half did so without. In some instances events were indeed recalled more accurately when using the LHC, but this was not always the case.
- Ellish et al. (1996) examined the reliability of self-reported sexual behavior in 162 heterosexual partnerships. Partners were enrolled on the same day and interviewed separately. The researchers collected information about sexual activity and condom use, using a LHC for the thirty days before enrolment. The agreement between the partners' answers was quite modest. The correlation coefficients between partner reports ranged from .43 for frequency of any sexual activity to .56 for the number of days on which vaginal intercourse occurred. Thus, it seems that the participants' reports were not very accurate, in spite of using a calendar.
- Finally, Goldman et al. (1998) administered a calendar to assess children's morbidity and treatment behavior during the two-week interval prior to the interviews with the participants (the parents) in their study. The results were quite similar to those reported in studies employing conventional questionnaire designs, although the data obtained offered a 'richer and more complex' description of child illness and treatment behavior.

Several other studies might have been mentioned here. However, the studies mentioned above illustrate aptly the results typically obtained in this kind of research: it seems fair to say that the LHC improves recall *sometimes* for *some* variables, but certainly not *always* for *all* variables. A prospective longitudinal design will virtually always result in better (more reliable and more accurate) data than a retrospective design. Of course, it may be impossible to circumvent asking retrospective questions: even in a panel study investigators must know what happened in between the waves of the study. However, it is recommended that retrospective questions be used sparingly, and that alternatives (such as increasing the number of

waves of a study or shortening the time lag between the waves of the study)
be carefully considered.

A related design: the cohort study

In his seminal paper, Norman B. Ryder defined 'cohort' as 'the aggregate
of individuals (within some population definition) who experienced the
same event within the same time interval' (1965: 845). One particularly
important type of cohort is the *birth cohort* – that is, the set of people who
were born in the same year. In the 1970s and early 1980s (which were, in
retrospect, the heydays of cohort research), about 90 per cent of the cohort
studies focused on birth cohorts (Glenn, 1981). However, other important
life events (including marriage, moment of entry on the labor market,
moment of diagnosis of a particular disease such as AIDS or cancer, etc.)
might also constitute a cohort.

Members of a particular cohort are assumed to experience the influence of
particular historical events in a similar manner, while members of different
cohorts are expected to be differentially affected by historical events. For
instance, Blossfeld (1993) documents the differential impact of World War
II, the following social and economic crises, and the rapid economic
recovery afterwards (the 'Wirtschaftswunder' – 'economic miracle' – of the
early 1960s) on the educational and vocational opportunities of members of
German birth cohorts 1916–65. He shows that especially the women of
birth cohorts 1929–31 carried the burden of the postwar crises. At age 17,
46 per cent of the males of this birth cohort enrolled in vocational training,
compared with only 20 per cent of the females (this figure was much higher
for older birth cohorts). Women of this cohort tended to enter the labor
market rather early and often in unskilled occupations, instead of receiving
lengthy vocational training or higher education. As a consequence, they
often lacked the educational qualifications necessary for later occupational
promotion (thus, to a certain degree, to profit from the Wirtschaftswunder).
Members of the older birth cohorts had already largely completed their
education with the onset of World War II, whereas younger birth cohorts
could profit from the social stability and economic growth of later years.
Clearly, historical circumstances experienced early in life severely affected
the educational and vocational opportunities of women of birth cohorts
1929–31.

Blossfeld's (1993) study shows how *external* events may differentially
affect the experiences of members of various birth cohorts. However, the
cohort variable can also be used as a proximate variable representing the
effects of the *internal* structure of cohorts, such as size and male/female
ratio. For example, war tends to result in a high female-to-male ratio for
particular birth cohorts, which may in turn affect the chances of females of

these cohorts to find a same-age partner, the timing and occurrence of childbirth, etc. Further, note that there may be classes of cohorts that are more or less similarly affected by historical events. Following Mannheim (1928/1929), these may be termed 'generations': groupings of cohorts characterized by a specific historical setting and by common characteristics on the individual (biographical characteristics, value orientations) and the systems level (size and composition, generational culture, Becker, 1993).

The Cohort variable must be distinguished from two related concepts. The first of these is *Age*. In cohort analysis, Age is measured as the amount of time elapsed since the cohort was constituted. For example, in the year 1997 the age of birth cohort 1962 was 35; in 2007, its age will be 45. The second related concept is *Period*. Operationally, this refers to the moment of observation. Like Cohort, Age and Period are not of much intrinsic interest to researchers: they are usually only measured because they present convenient and readily measurable indicators of more basic 'underlying' concepts. For example, cohort Age may represent concepts such as maturation and biological or intellectual development (for birth cohorts), vocational career phase (for labor market cohorts), etc. Similarly, the meaning of the Period concept is much wider than its simple measurement suggests. It refers to all events relevant to the issue of concern that have occurred between the waves of the study.

The rather diffuse and imprecise measurements of the concepts that underlie the Age, Period, and Cohort variables pose the problem that the effects of these variables can rarely be interpreted unambiguously; other interpretations are often quite plausible as well (Rodgers, 1982). For example, a researcher may argue that a significant Period effect is due to historical event *A*; critics, however, might feel that events *B* or *C* (that happened to coincide with event *A*) are more likely to be responsible for this result. As Costa and McCrae (1982) warned, an ageing effect is not equivalent to a maturational effect – but how can we distinguish between these two interpretations if only cohort Age has been measured?

Further, cohort research is hampered by the fact that at the operational level the three concepts of Age, Period and Cohort are linearly dependent. Once a person's scores on two of these variables is known, the score on the third variable follows automatically: Age equals Period minus Cohort. This implies that statistically it is impossible to identify the effects of all three variables in the same analysis, although it is often theoretically of great interest to distinguish among them.

Three main strategies have been proposed to solve this problem. Mason et al. (1973) noted that operationally one may impose constraints on any of the three Age/Period/Cohort (APC) variables, without affecting the underlying theoretical framework. For example, two or more birth cohorts might be combined into one 'generation', presuming that the members of these cohorts experienced the events of interest in a similar manner. At the operational level, such a constraint resolves the linear dependency among the APC variables, meaning that the effects of the APC variables can be identified simultaneously. Simple as this may sound, this strategy does have its drawbacks. Although the linear dependency among the APC variables disappears after imposing a particular constraint, the statistical association among the three variables usually remains high. The estimates of the effects of the three APC variables are therefore highly dependent on the constraints chosen; different restrictions often radically change the outcomes of the study. Thus, it seems important that researchers employing this strategy present theoretical arguments as to why a particular constraint is 'right'.

Further, researchers may limit their attention to just two of the three APC variables. One may consider all two-way Age–Period–Cohort combinations pairwisely in the same study. Thus, three analyses are conducted, concerning Age–Period effects, Age–Cohort effects, and Period–Cohort effects, respectively (see Schaie, 1965, and Schaie and Herzog, 1982, for more formal discussions of this approach). This strategy was quite popular in the late 1970s as it solves the dependency among the APC variables. However, the difficulties in interpreting the effects still remain.

Finally, Rodgers (1982) urged scientists to replace the proximate concepts of Age, Period and Cohort by their underlying concepts. For instance, whereas Age might be taken to represent intellectual development, it would make more sense to measure intellectual development using an appropriate psychological test. This strategy resolves the two problems discussed above simultaneously. Interpretation of effects becomes much easier when the concepts in question are measured directly, rather than through a proximate variable. The linear dependency among the APC variables disappears if even one of them is measured in terms of the underlying variable. Unfortunately, this strategy has only limited applicative potential. First, it is more costly (in terms of time and resources) to measure, say, intellectual development by means of a multi-item psychological test than by cohort Age. Second, this strategy is only feasible in prospective studies. It cannot be applied if one re-analyzes data that were collected several decades ago – yet, the great attraction of many cohort studies is that they combine data from past and present studies, and put these in a new perspective.

Many of the designs that were discussed in this chapter may provide data that can be arranged such as to allow for an APC analysis. That is, data from separate cross-sectional studies, intervention studies, panel studies, and trend studies may freely be merged, as long as the concept of interest is measured more or less similarly across the studies to be included in the analysis. Measures of subject age (Age) and year of birth (Cohort) are virtually always available, or can be inferred. The year in which a particular study was conducted constitutes the Period variable. In this fashion, it is usually quite easy to create a data matrix that is suitable for APC analysis.

A checklist

This chapter discussed the basic design issues in longitudinal research. By way of a summary, I provide a short checklist of what should be clear (or, at the very least, which issues should have been considered) before undertaking a longitudinal study.

- The first important issue refers to the *objectives* of the study. Is it sufficient to examine the covariation among the variables under study, or does one aim to examine causal relationships? If the latter applies, a research design that yields longitudinal data (that is, data covering a period of time, not just the state of things at one particular moment in time) is very desirable. However, keep in mind that many issues can be studied quite well by means of a cross-sectional design. As was seen earlier on, a cross-sectional design allows for a test of the association among the variables of interest, and it can also provide information regarding the possible spuriousness of an association. A longitudinal design improves on a cross-sectional design only in that it provides information about the order of the variables of interest; the value of such information has been questioned, however.
- Given the objectives of the study, one must consider the *basic design* of the study. It may be unnecessary to repeatedly interview the same set of participants; a repeated cross-sectional design or a retrospective design might do. However, a longitudinal design is indispensable if information is needed about change on the level of the research units.
- If a prospective longitudinal design is selected as the design that suits one's needs best, one has to decide about the *number of waves* and the *spacing between these*. The number of waves of the study is often dictated by the available resources. It might be possible to extend the number of waves by interviewing fewer participants than intended, but that may be a risky matter, given that there will be at least some nonresponse. The spacing between the waves is an important matter, as results tend to change with varying periods of time between the waves of a study (Sandefur and Tuma, 1987). This issue is elaborated in Chapter 4. Further, the rate of change of the variable(s) of interest will also be relevant (Campbell, 1988).
- In prospective longitudinal designs, the investigator must decide about the *variables to be included in the study*, as well as about the *time of measurement* of these variables. Some concepts vary across participants, but not across time (e.g., year of birth, gender; many personality variables are assumed to be stable across the life course). It is convenient to measure such concepts at the start of the study, as they will usually be used to predict change in other, less stable variables in the study. They may be omitted from later waves of the study.

occasions of measurement (how many, how often)
variables
sample size

- Obviously, the investigator must decide about the *size of the sample* that one would like to have. Given that the nonresponse in any particular study is virtually always higher than initially expected, prudent researchers will maximize the target sample size, given the number of waves that are minimally needed for providing answers to the research questions.

    Researchers sometimes feel that there is a trade-off between the number of participants to be included in their study and the number of waves of the study. The money saved by confining to a lower sample size could for example be spent on an extra wave. Actually, this reasoning is incorrect. The sample size needed for the first wave of a longitudinal study increases with the number of waves of that study, because people have more opportunities to drop out of the study in a multi-wave study than in a two-wave study. Thus, if anything, adding an extra wave to a study means that the sample size at the first wave of the study must be increased (see also Chapter 2).

Further reading

The issue of study design has received quite some attention. Almost any introductory text book on research methods contains a section (or even a chapter) on this issue. However, *longitudinal* research designs usually receive very little attention. For example, Robson's otherwise excellent introduction to research methods in the behavioral and social sciences devotes just a few lines to longitudinal research, stating that it '. . . tends to be difficult to carry out and is demanding on the time and resources of the investigator' (1993: 50). Cook and D.T. Campbell's (1979) classic text is more useful in this respect, in that it provides much understanding of the relationships between the target of a study and its design. R.T. Campbell (1988) provides also a checklist of sorts.

    As regards the reliability and validity of retrospective reports, Schwarz and Sudman (1994) provide a thorough and yet accessible discussion of these issues. From a somewhat different angle I might also recommend Elizabeth Loftus's work on false recovered memories. Her work is very instructive regarding the workings of the human mind, from which it can be inferred that one should not put too much faith in the accuracy of others' (or one's own) memory.

2 Nonresponse in Longitudinal Research

The current chapter discusses the issue of nonresponse in both cross-sectional and longitudinal research designs. After distinguishing between random and nonrandom (or selective) nonresponse, I address strategies to improve response rates. Successively I discuss methods to detect non-random nonresponse, and post-hoc strategies to correct for selectivity. Further, I deal with methods for handling missing data and attrition. I conclude that the bias resulting from selective nonresponse is difficult to correct, so that every possible effort should be made to improve response rates.

Nonresponse in cross-sectional and longitudinal designs

In virtually every survey, only part of the sample that was initially drawn actually takes part in the study. Interviewers may be unable to contact some people; a potential participant's language command might be below par, or his or her mental state may prohibit participation; others will simply refuse to cooperate. Since the 1950s, nonresponse has gradually become a major problem in survey research. By now, nonresponse rates in the range of 30 to 40 per cent are quite common. Goyder (1987) found in his extensive review of 312 mail, face-to-face, and telephone surveys, that the nonresponse in these was on average 41.6, 32.7, and 39.8 per cent, respectively. Similar findings, albeit based on only 45 studies, were reported by Hox and De Leeuw (1994).

A report of the American Statistical Association (1974) identified two major reasons for the increasing nonresponse rates. First, contact rates have detoriated as a result of the growing tendency for entire families to be away from home when interviewers call. This is due to demographic factors like the increasing proportions of dual-earner couples and people living alone, and the additional amount of time spent commuting (Kessler et al., 1995).

Second, cooperation rates have declined across time. For example, Steeh (1981) reported that refusal rates in two ongoing trend studies conducted by a major American university survey research center increased from a mere 6–8 per cent in the 1950s to 15–20 per cent by the end of the 1970s. Goyder (1987) speculated that the increase in refusal rates is due to people's decreasing sense of social responsibility, in conjunction with a general decrease in the cohesion of society and less belief in the legitimacy of social institutions. Further, the number of surveys has increased dramatically over the years, up to the point that many people (at least in the Western world) are asked to participate in at least one survey per year. Moreover, being a survey participant is not always fun (answer a survey question about old-age savings today, and you may find an insurance agent on your doorstep tomorrow), which may lower people's inclination to participate in future surveys (Kessler et al., 1995). Smith (1995) argues that, in so far as there is a trend towards lower response rates (which he doubts), this is probably due to procedural and methodological changes, such as the increased use of telephone surveys (which on average yield a higher nonresponse rate than face-to-face interviews). Finally, increasing concerns about privacy and confidentiality may also have contributed to the decreasing response rates.

Selective nonresponse

High response rates are important for two reasons. One is that a decrease in response rates translates directly into an increase in the number of people to be contacted, and, hence, in an increase in the costs of the study. Given a fixed budget to be spent on data collection, a high nonresponse rate thus yields a correspondingly lower sample size, which in turn reduces the precision of survey estimates. However, this is just a minor problem compared with the risk that nonresponse is *not random* or *selective*. Responders and nonresponders may differ systematically on the variables of interest, leading to a sample that is not representative for the target group (a 'biased' sample). Conclusions based on analyses conducted on a biased sample cannot be generalized to the target population. It is obviously difficult to say something meaningful about groups that were hardly represented in the sample, but even if the overall response rate is high, the bias in the sample may be substantial if responders differ considerably from nonresponders. A high response rate can mitigate the problems that follow from a potentially selective nonresponse, in that nonresponse can only be problematic to the degree that there *is* any.

Nonresponse analysis typically reveals at least some differences between the responders and nonresponders in a study. The four examples below illustrate the differences that may occur.

- Kreiger and Nishri (1997) examined the nonresponse in a case-control study on renal cell carcinoma conducted in Ontario. In a case-control study, 'cases' (those who possess a characteristic of interest to the researcher – in this case, persons who have been diagnosed as having renal cancer) are coupled to 'controls' (persons who are identical to the cases in a number of important respects, except for the characteristic of interest). Kreiger and Nishri found that cases, women, persons under 60, and persons living in a rural area were more likely to respond.

- Mihelic and Crimmins (1997) examined the loss to follow-up in a sample of older Americans (aged 70 and over). Persons of older ages, lower education, who lived alone, and have more functioning impairments were more likely to become nonresponders.

- Martin (1994) manipulated the 'level of interest' of a study experimentally. Half of the participants of an amateur bowling tournament were mailed a high-interest version of a questionnaire, whereas the other half received a low-interest version. The two versions differed in the presumed topic of the study, but were identical in all other respects. The persons in the high-interest condition were almost twice as likely to respond than those in the low-interest condition.

- In a four-wave study on parental mental health problems following stillbirth, neonatal death or sudden infant death syndrome, Boyle et al. (1996) found that younger, unmarried, and unemployed fathers and mothers without private health insurance were less often recruited for the study; if recruited, they were more likely to drop out.

Although these examples are atypical on their own, in conjunction they are fairly representative for the findings obtained in nonresponse research. The 'average' survey nonresponder is a poorly educated, unmarried male who is either quite young or quite old. He lives in an urban neighborhood, may have mental and/or physical health problems, and he could definitely not care less about the topic of the survey – surely not an easy target! Is it really worth the trouble to spend scarce resources trying to interview such persons? Or, what are the potential consequences of nonrandom nonresponse?

Grimsmo et al.'s (1981) study on the effectiveness of self-help groups provides a good example of the impact of selective nonresponse. In Norway, self-help groups for weight control have grown into a nation-wide movement with some 80,000 people participating. They work in groups of 8–12 people, meeting once a week for eight weeks, monitoring body weight each time. The drop-out rate is less than 10 per cent. In a prospective study, Grimsmo et al. obtained data on initial weight, weight at weekly intervals, and end results of 11,410 individuals. The average weight loss of the 10,650 participants who completed the course (93.3 per cent of the initial group) was 6.9 kg. With the drop-outs included (and assuming these had not lost any weight), the average weight loss was smaller (6.4 kg). Although even this latter figure is impressive, these findings suggest that there were considerable differences between the participants who stayed in the study and those who dropped out, leading to an overestimation of the effectiveness of self-help groups if the drop-out is not taken into consideration.

This example shows that selective nonresponse may present a serious threat to the validity of one's conclusions. This does not apply only if the investigator is interested in examining means and averages (as in the Grimsmo et al. study). Selective nonresponse may also have severe effects on the associations between pairs of variables. Sampling bias usually results in a sample that is more homogeneous in respect to particular variables than the target population; if males tend to drop out of the study, females will be overrepresented in the final sample. A strongly biased sample consists of many people who are basically of the same kind, at least regarding the variables that were related to the variables determining nonresponse. If there is only little variation on a particular variable, it becomes hard to find statistically-significant relationships between this variable and other variables. Moreover, even *if* a relationship is found, this relationship may well be biased (the association between two variables would then be different from the relation that would have been found, had the sample been representative, Goodman and Blum, 1996). The amount of bias depends both on the degree to which nonresponse was selective (the difference between the characteristics of responders and nonresponders), and the strength of the association between the factors determining selective nonresponse and the variables of interest.

Nonresponse and attrition in longitudinal research

The reasons for minimizing nonresponse in cross-sectional studies (reduction of the costs of data collection, and the possibility of selectiveness) apply to longitudinal research designs as well. We can distinguish among several types of nonresponse in longitudinal research. *Initial nonresponse* occurs when the missing values are located at the beginning of the study; this occurs when people contacted for the first wave of the study refuse (or are unable) to participate, while they do participate in later waves of the study. This type of nonresponse does not occur very frequently; usually the investigator takes a refusal for granted, the implicit assumption being that people would have found the time to be interviewed if they had been really interested in participating in the study.

The missing values may also be located at the end of the study; this is called *attrition*. Attrition occurs when respondents leave the panel after having participated in one or more consecutive waves of the study, including the first. These respondents are not contacted for later waves. Thus, attrition is cumulative; once a participant has missed one of the waves, s/he is lost for the remainder of the study.

amount of
bias depends on:
① selection effects (of non-response)
② strength of association between selection factors
    and variables

Types of longitudinal non-response
① initial
② attrition
  – may be wave-related

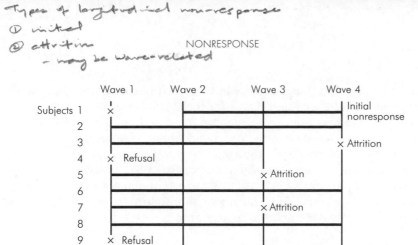

Figure 2.1   *Nonresponse and panel attrition in a four-wave panel study*

Wave nonresponse refers to a situation in which a particular respondent participates in some, but not all waves of the study. Thus, wave non-response does not necessarily mean that the participant is lost for all waves of the study; it is neither structural nor cumulative. For example, a person may have participated in the first and third wave, but not in the second wave of a study.

Note that in practice the terms 'nonresponse' and 'attrition' are often used interchangeably. As the exposé above has made clear, this is not entirely correct; although attrition is the most frequently occurring form of nonresponse in longitudinal studies, other types of nonresponse may occur as well. Figure 2.1 illustrates the differences among these types of non-response graphically. Only persons 2, 6 and 8 in Figure 2.1 participated in all four waves of the study. The other persons all missed at least one of the waves (denoted by an '×'). Persons 4 and 9 explicitly refused to participate in the study at the first wave, and were not contacted further (refusal). Person 1 was unable to participate in the first wave of the study, but participated in all later waves (initial nonresponse). The remaining subjects (3, 5 and 7) completed at least one of the waves of the study, but dropped out and did not return in the panel (panel attrition).

Figure 2.1 also presents an example of the impact of cumulative non-response in longitudinal research designs. If we were to compute the time-1 to time-4 stability of a particular variable across time for the data presented in Figure 2.1, only participants 2, 6 and 8 would be included in the study – the information obtained for the other participants would be useless. Cumulative nonresponse can greatly reduce the size of the final sample. If the chance that a person will participate in any particular wave of a four-wave study is .8, only (.8^4 equals) 41 per cent of the respondents of the first wave will have remained in the study after four waves – a figure that is not exceptionally low (compare Van de Pol, 1989). Thus, researchers should not be overly optimistic about the response rates in their own research, and they should aim at reasonably large sample sizes for the first wave of their study.

Small sample size, however, is not the most serious threat that follows from a high nonresponse rate. As stated above, responders may differ systematically and in important respects from nonresponders. As non-response can only be selective to the degree that there *is* nonresponse, one 'standard piece of advice' (Little, 1995) is that nonresponse should be avoided wherever possible. Therefore, the following section addresses strategies that may be employed to this aim.

Better safe than sorry: minimizing nonresponse and attrition

Investigators can adopt two basic approaches to the reduction of non-response and attrition. One is to use data collection strategies that improve contact rates. The other concerns the application of strategies aiming to reduce the number of refusals.

Improving contact rates

As was seen earlier on, noncontact rates have increased over the last few decades. Increased field effort may meet this type of nonresponse. For example, Kessler et al. (1995) describe the strategies used for the National Comorbidity Study (NCS). The NCS was a large-scale national survey carried out in 1990–92 to examine the prevalence, causes, and consequences of psychiatric morbidity and comorbidity in the United States. Measures taken to increase contact rates included use of a *very long field period* and an *extended callback schedule* in an effort to minimize the number of potential respondents who could not be contacted. Further, at the last wave of the study, *hard-to-reach households were undersampled* by half, and twice as much field effort was devoted in each case to making contacts with the remaining half-sample during the last month of the field period.

The primary reason for attrition during follow-up waves in longitudinal studies is that interviewers are unable to contact people who participated in earlier waves of the study (American Statistical Association, 1974). For example, it can be difficult to trace respondents who have moved between the waves of the study. Freedman et al. (1990) present extensive reviews of strategies to trace such participants, such as consulting municipal registers, contacting employers or the current inhabitants of the former address of the participant, and so on. Such strategies may be quite effective. For example, Ellickson et al. (1988) used some of these strategies in a longitudinal study of adolescent behavior to trace a group of highly mobile junior high school transferees. Students were tracked through the home or the new school.

When students were tracked through the latter route, surveys were sent directly to the school itself instead of asking for a home mailing address, thus avoiding asking school officials to give out personal information, and enhanced the likelihood of the survey being delivered. The tracking efforts cut nonresponse attributable to between-school mobility by 66 per cent, and reduced the attrition rate by 50 per cent.

One easy way to trace respondents who have moved is to ask participants at the end of an interview to provide names and addresses of two or three persons who may be able to tell the researchers where the respondents are, in case they cannot be contacted for a follow-up. This strategy is particularly efficient if the respondent belongs to a population that has a high mobility rate. The 'backup' names and addresses must belong to people who can be expected to have a lower mobility rate than the respondents themselves. For example, backup names and addresses of friends and acquaintances may be of little use in a study among highly mobile young adults (the backup persons being as mobile as the respondents themselves), whereas their parents' addresses may be far more helpful.

Reducing the number of refusals

There is a natural limit to the effectiveness of strategies aiming at improving contact rates, as some surveys already have contact rates close to 100 per cent. In such cases, the issue is how to persuade people to participate, rather than how to contact them. It is illuminating to construe the decision to participate in a study as the outcome of a rational decision process in which the expected 'costs' of participation (for example, the time that might be spent on other activities) and 'rewards' (such as the feeling that one is doing their duty, gifts to be received after the questionnaire has been completed) play an important role (Hox et al., 1995). If the rewards exceed the costs, the participant will cooperate; if the costs are higher than the rewards, a refusal will follow. This suggests two basic ways of reducing refusal rates. One is to increase the participants' (perceived) rewards; the other is to lower their (perceived) costs.

Increasing rewards   The relationship between an investigator and the participants recruited for the study is often a one-sided affair. The respondents provide the investigator with information about what they feel, think and do; but what do they get in return? Some of them may be flattered by the interviewer's interest, but for many others the mere fact that someone wants their cooperation is no sufficient reason to participate. Several measures have been proposed to secure the cooperation of such people.

First, people participating in a study must feel that the information they provide is really appreciated. One way of doing this is by 'flattering' the respondents, telling them that their participation is important for the study (as a matter of fact, their participation *is* important – no undue compliments here). For example, one of Thornton et al.'s (1982) interviewers persuaded respondents to participate in a follow-up wave by calling them, saying 'Most of the respondents consider us old friends. Many were waiting for our call, wondering if they would ever hear from us again. We have shown in the past that we really care about what they think'. Would anyone dare say 'no' to this interviewer? Similarly, Maynard (1996) tested the assumption that ingratiation through the researcher's frank request for compliance yields higher response rates to mail surveys. The experimental group was given a questionnaire in which a cartoon of the researcher 'begging' the recipient to respond was inserted, while the control group received the same questionnaire without this cartoon. As expected, a reduction in nonresponse rates was achieved within the treatment group.

As words (cartoons) are cheap, the message that the investigator really values one's cooperation becomes easier to believe if this 'psychological incentive' is accompanied by a gift coupon or a small present (Church, 1993). Groenland and Van de Stadt (1985) experimented with a reward for respondents who completed a particular interview in a panel study. Two hundred households in the socio-economic panel of the Dutch Census were promised a gift coupon and a bathing towel (total value US$20), while another two hundred households were neither promised nor given a reward. The response in the rewarded group was 62 per cent, while the corresponding figure in the control group was 48 per cent. The willingness to participate in future waves of the same study was also higher in the rewarded group (93 versus 84 per cent, respectively). Findings like these suggest that the extra costs involved in rewarding participants may well be offset by higher participation rates. Note, however, that professional organizations such as the British Psychological Society prohibit using incentives to induce participants to risk harm beyond that which they risk without such incentives in their normal lifestyle (British Psychological Society, 1991).

Incentives can take on several forms. Instead of giving all responders a small reward, investigators may hold lotteries among them. Rather than the certainty that they will receive a small reward, participants have a – considerably smaller – chance to win a large reward. Many variations on this theme can be devised, depending on the available resources, but also on the characteristics of the population. For instance, a small amount of money may not improve response rates among well-paid and extremely busy CEOs, while it could be highly effective in a sample of (usually poor) students. This idea was supported in a study by Schweitzer and Asch (1995), who showed that people with lower salaries were more likely to respond when paid for their cooperation than those with higher salaries. This suggests that incentives will be effective only if they are proportionate to the subjective effort asked from the participants. Indeed, if people feel that the value of the incentive *under*values their time, the response rate may actually decrease (Kessler et al., 1995).

Many people who participate in a survey are eager to know the results of the study. Researchers can use this to their advantage with an eye to improving response rates, by telling participants that they will be informed about the results of the study. The feedback may take the form of a small report to be sent to the participants, summarizing the most interesting results ('interesting' to be participants, that is). From the participants' view, such a report is an incentive in its own right. Further, this approach provides the investigators with an opportunity to check whether the addresses in their database are still correct. If a respondent has moved only recently, it is much easier to trace this person than in a later stage of the study. One may even include change of address cards with the report, to be returned free of charge to the survey institute in case one has moved (Dijkstra and Smit, 1993).

Costs of participating in a panel study   Understandably, response rates tend to decrease if providing the requested information demands great efforts from the respondents. One obvious 'cost' is the *amount of time needed to participate* in the study (e.g., to complete the questionnaire, to talk to the interviewer). Response rates tend to vary inversely with questionnaire length; short questionnaires yield high response rates. In a study on women and cancer conducted among 1,000 Norwegian women aged 35–49 years, Lund and Gram (1998) found that their two-page questionnaire yielded a 70.2 per cent response rate, while four- and six-page versions of this questionnaire resulted in 62.8 and 63.3 per cent response rates, respectively. In a similar vein, Eaker et al. (1998) found that the likelihood that people responded to a short version of their questionnaire was about 24 per cent higher than the likelihood of responding to the long version of this questionnaire. Finally, Burchell and Marsh (1992) administered a lengthy questionnaire to 300 English and Scottish adults, and obtained a very low 15 per cent response rate. Follow-up interviews with the nonresponders revealed that questionnaire length had been the primary reason for not responding (this sounds paradoxical, but many nonresponders can be persuaded to participate when offered a fitting incentive. For example, nonresponders in the National Comorbidity Survey were offered a $100 reward if they participated in a 20-minute screening interview – the participants receiving only $20 and a commemorative pen, Kessler et al., 1995).

These examples show that it is a good idea to keep your questionnaire as short as possible. For mail questionnaires, a maximum length of eleven pages has been suggested (Dillman, 1978), but the response rate in the Lund and Gram study discussed above already detoriated when the participants had to complete a four-page rather than a two-page questionnaire.

No corresponding rules of thumb are available for interview length, but common sense suggests that response rates in long interviews will be lower than in short interviews.

Apart from the time needed to participate, there are also other costs associated with survey participation. The *topic of the study may be uninteresting* or irrelevant to some. As mentioned above, Martin (1994) showed that the high-interest version of his questionnaire resulted in a much higher response than a low-interest version. Differential levels of study interest / study relevance might also account for the results reported by Lund and Gram (1998), who examined the effects of questionnaire title on response rates. In their study among 1,000 Norwegian women, a 70.2 per cent response rate was obtained for a questionnaire titled 'Women and cancer'. An in other respects identical questionnaire titled 'Oral contraceptives and cancer' yielded a 10 per cent lower response rate. One explanation for this result is that not all women in the sample used oral contraceptives, and that these women felt that this survey was irrelevant to them. Thus, lack of personal relevance may have led them to become nonresponders.

Furthermore, the *topic of the study may be psychologically threatening*. Gmel (1996) found in a study on alcohol consumption that heavy drinkers often refused to participate in the section of a questionnaire addressing alcohol consumption (abstainers, however, were also less likely to respond to this section, perhaps because some of them were former alcohol addicts). Similarly, Catania et al. (1986) found in a study on sexual behavior that partial responders failed to answer sexuality questions (e.g., frequency of masturbating) because they were uneasy making personal disclosures of sexual information. This result also touches on the issue of the *confidentiality* of the respondents' answers. It is commonly assumed that assurances of confidentiality result in higher response rates, but this seems only partially true. Singer et al.'s (1995) meta-analysis showed that stronger assurance of confidentiality did in general not yield higher response rates. However, if the data asked about were sensitive, a small but significant effect in the expected direction was observed.

Finally, there are two important measures for improving response rates that do not readily fit the costs–rewards framework outlined above. First, *preliminary notification* usually leads to higher retrieval rates. Many large-scale surveys use advance letters in which potential respondents are notified that they will be contacted to participate in the study. Such letters usually contain information about the organization conducting the study, the rationale and purpose of the study, along with information about how the respondent was selected. Eaker et al. (1998) estimated that in their study preliminary notification led to a 30 per cent higher retrieval rate. Further, *reminders* are often used to improve response rates. Nederhof (1988) reported that telephone reminders were as effective in boosting response rates as certified mailings; both reduced nonresponse rates by 34 per cent.

Detecting selective nonresponse

Earlier on I addressed the possible impact of selective nonresponse, and discussed strategies to minimize nonresponse rates. Although consistent use of these strategies may increase response rates, in survey research it is unavoidable that at least some nonresponse occurs. Given the potential impact of selective nonresponse on the validity of a study, investigators must examine the nonresponse that has occurred with an eye to potential bias. This section discusses three strategies that may be employed to that aim. These are (a) comparison of key figures on the composition of the sample with corresponding figures that are known for the target population, or for earlier research in which similar variables were measured; (b) comparison of responders and nonresponders; and (c) inspection of the nonresponse pattern.

Figures on the composition of the target population

One approach to obtaining insight into the degree to which a sample is biased is to compare figures on the composition of the target population to the distributions of the corresponding variables in the sample. In many national censuses information is collected about key figures for the population (such as age, gender, marital and employment status, income, and level of education). This information is often available to the general public, usually in the form of frequency distributions, means and standard deviations, and the like. Such population figures can be compared with the corresponding figures obtained for the sample. If the sample figures differ from the population figures, the sample is not representative for this population. The reverse, however, does not hold: if no differences are found, it does not follow that the sample is representative for the population. Sample–population comparisons include usually only a limited number of variables. Even if there are no differences for the variables under study, there may be major differences between the population and the sample for other concepts.

Further, for many variables of interest no population distributions are known. It is sometimes possible to compare figures obtained for one's own sample to those from earlier studies that focused on similar research issues. These may then serve as a standard against which one can judge one's own sample. For example, if you find that about 60 per cent of the adult population is lonely (an extremely high figure, which casts doubts on the validity of the instruments used as well as the representativeness of the sample), your claims become more credible if authors X, Y and Z also found that about 60 per cent of the adult population was lonely. The difficulty with this approach is that such other studies do not present an *objective* benchmark – that is, it remains unknown what the population

Table 2.1 *Marginals cannot yield conclusive evidence about representativeness*

(a) Strong association between variables				(b) Independence of variables		
cells	Employed	Not employed	*Marginals*		Employed	Not employed
Male	.10	.40	.50	Male	.25	.25	.50
Female	.40	.10	.50	Female	.25	.25	.50
	.50	.50			.50	.50

figures actually are. If there is no difference between your study and the comparison study, yours might be just as bad as the comparison study as regards the nonresponse. Indeed, differences might signal either that your study is better – or even worse – than the comparison study.

Finally, it is one thing to focus on means and variances. It is reassuring to confirm that your sample is in a number of respects 'representative' for the target population, because comparison of these did not reveal important differences between them. However, even if sample and target population are comparable in terms of the means and standard deviations of the variables in the study, it might still well be that important differences have not been detected. For instance, assume that half of a particular population is male, and that half of this population is employed. There are many cross-classifications that are compatible with these assumptions. Table 2.1 presents two examples. In Table 2.1(a), there is a strong association between gender and employment status; in Table 2.1(b) these two variables are independent. Were we to compare only the marginal distributions of gender and employment status, we would conclude that there are no major differences between these two distributions. Clearly, a sample may differ strongly from a target population, even if the univariate distributions with regard to particular variables are identical (Goodman and Blum, 1996).

Summarizing, comparison of the marginal frequencies of the sample to those obtained for the population may be quite useful, in that the hypothesis that there are no differences between population and sample can be falsified. Conversely, this approach cannot be used to argue that the sample is representative for a particular population.

Comparison of responders and nonresponders

Another way to test for selective nonresponse is to examine the differences between responders and nonresponders. This type of analysis typically takes the form of a multivariate analysis of variance (MANOVA), in which the responders are compared with the nonresponders regarding their average scores on study variables. For example, if the responders and nonresponders do not differ in terms of age and gender, the representativeness of the sample has not worsened in these respects. The weaknesses of this approach are that investigators still have to test for the representativeness of the sample at the first occasion, while it may still be the case that if other variables were to have been examined, a significant association between these and the likelihood of responding would have been found. Again, this type of approach cannot yield conclusive evidence as to whether the sample is representative.

Inspection of nonresponse patterns

Nonresponse rates need not be the same for all waves of a longitudinal study. Indeed, nonresponse rates frequently decrease with every successive wave. Consider the nonresponse rates in the three-wave study among Dutch youth reported by Taris (1996, 1997). The nonresponse rates for the three waves were 37, 20, and 11 per cent for each successive wave. One reason might have been that the participants took more pleasure in completing the questionnaires with every successive wave, or that their commitment to the study increased across time – nothing to worry about. Unfortunately, a decreasing nonresponse rate may also indicate severe problems with respect to the representativeness of the sample.

Assume that a population consists of two groups (A and B) of equal size, which have a different chance to participate in the study. The likelihood to participate (the *response probability*) is, say, .9 for members of group A and .6 for members of group B. Further, let the chance to be asked to participate in the study be equal for both groups. How many people must be contacted to obtain a 1,000 person sample for the first wave of the study, and how will the composition of this sample change for each successive wave, assuming that the respective response probabilities are constant over time? These questions can be answered by solving the equations

$$.9 \ A + .6 \ B = 1{,}000 \qquad (2.1a)$$
$$A = B \qquad (2.1b)$$

showing that in total 1,334 persons (667 of each group) must be contacted for a 1,000-person sample. Of the 667 persons belonging to group A, 600 (90 per cent) will participate in the first wave of the study. However, at that time the sample will include only 400 members of group B (60 per cent of 667). Thus, at the first wave of the study there are 1.5 members of group A for each member of group B. Figure 2.2 shows that the overrepresentation of members of group A increases with every successive wave. At the fourth wave there are five members of group A to one member of group B. Obviously, the sample is strongly biased after four waves, and the chance

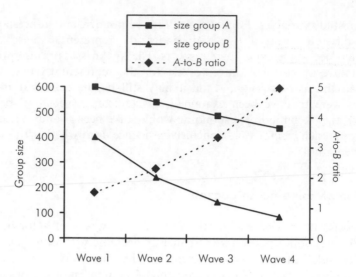

Figure 2.2   *Selective nonresponse at work: the relation between response rates and the overrepresentation of groups, for four waves and two groups A and B with response probabilities .9 and .6*

that the analyses conducted on this sample yield ill-found conclusions is considerable. This, of course, also depends on the magnitude of the differences between members of group A and B: if A's and B's are identical in all respects save group membership and response probability, conclusions are unlikely to be biased.

Note that the nonresponse in the example presented in Figure 2.2 decreases across waves. The nonresponse percentages are 25.0, 22.0, 19.2, and 16.7 for each successive wave. This is because group A (whose members make up a larger part of the sample with every wave) has a higher response rate than B. If the number of waves were to become infinitely large, the response rate for the total sample would ultimately become .9, because all members of group B would have left the study.

This example shows that the nonresponse in samples consisting of groups with different response probabilities will decrease across time. This suggests that selective nonresponse can be detected by inspecting the nonresponse patterns across time: the steeper the decline in nonresponse rates, the more likely it becomes that the sample is getting biased.

Dealing with nonresponse

It is unlikely that there will be no attrition at all in a longitudinal study, even if some or all of the measures discussed in this chapter are adopted.

Hence, some degree of incompleteness of the data is inevitable; but how should we deal with such missing data? The answer to this question partly depends on the structure of the process that generated the missing data. It is convenient to distinguish among three types of nonresponse (Little and Rubin, 1990). Assume that variable X has been completely observed, whereas variable Y has several missing values. One possibility is that the probability of obtaining a missing value for Y depends on neither X nor Y. That is, a participant's score on X does not predict whether this person's score on Y is missing; whereas it is also not the case that persons with score y on variable Y are more likely to have a missing value on Y (for example, if Y is depression, and depressive and non-depressive persons have the same likelihood to have a missing value on this variable). If these two requirements are satisfied, the missing values are randomly distributed across the cases; the missing values are *missing completely at random* (abbreviated as MCAR). In a longitudinal context, people may have a missing value for Y because they dropped out of the study. If this attrition is not systematically related to any (measured or unmeasured) variable, the missing values are MCAR, and the nonresponse mechanism can be neglected: no special measures need to be taken during the analysis of the data.

Another possibility is that the probability of obtaining a missing value for Y depends on the value of X, but not on the value of Y. For example, suppose that Y is income, X is socio-economic status, and that individuals with a high socio-economic status are more likely to have a missing value on income. As X is always observed, the missing values on Y are *missing at random* (MAR); the missing values are not MCAR, because the value of Y is missing conditionally on the value of X. In longitudinal settings, drop out is MAR if it depends completely on observed values of a particular variable (Diggle and Kenward, 1994; Little, 1995). For example, assume that the attrition in a study is completely accounted for by gender. Although this means that attrition was selective (e.g., the nonresponse was higher among males than among females), attrition was MAR *within* each gender category. If the data are MAR, the nonresponse mechanism can also be neglected.

Finally, the missing values for Y may depend on the values of both X and Y. If Y is income and individuals with a high income are more likely to have a missing value than others, then the missing values are not MAR. In practice, it is often difficult to decide whether the missing values are MAR or not. In the case of income, information about the participants' job level may be useful in determining whether missing values on income are MAR. Job level is usually positively correlated with income, and explains about a quarter of the variance in income. If participants with a high-level job are more likely to have a missing value on income, it seems likely that these missings are not MAR. If the missing values are neither MCAR nor MAR, the nonresponse mechanism *cannot* be neglected, and measures must be taken in the data analysis phase (see below).

Analyzing incomplete data

There are three general strategies for analyzing incomplete data (Little and Rubin, 1987, 1990). These are imputation of missing values, weighting of cases, and direct analysis of the incomplete data. *Imputation* replaces missing values by more or less suitable estimates, then proceeds by analyzing the data as if there were no missings in the data. This strategy primarily aims to deal with nonresponse when there are missing values at some of the items. This procedure is attractive, because cases that would be discarded if the analysis were restricted to the complete cases are retained, whereas the resulting complete data can be analyzed using standard software packages.

There are several well-known procedures to impute missing values. Possibly the most popular of these is to fill in the mean value of a particular variable (computed across the cases without missing values on this variable) for the missings on this variable (this strategy is also termed *unconditional mean imputation*, Little and Rubin, 1990). Alternatively, one may impute an estimate of the mean of the conditional distribution of X_2, given X_1 is imputed. An often used subform of this *conditional mean imputation* is *regression imputation*, where the regression of X_2 on X_1 is used to impute the conditional mean of the missing X_2 values. That is, a missing x_{i2} is replaced by its prediction $\hat{x}_{i2}$ from the regression of X_2 on X_1:

$$\hat{x}_{i2} = a + b_1 X_1, \tag{2.3}$$

where a is an intercept and b_1 the unstandardized regression estimate for the effect of X_1 on X_2. Note that more than one predictor variable may be included. This method is especially acceptable if most of the variance of X_2 is accounted for by X_1 (as often occurs in longitudinal research; many variables are rather stable across time; compare Chapters 3 and 4).

Both types of imputation are good for estimating means, but not for estimating variances and covariances. Imputing the mean of a variable for all missing cases on this variable (what Little and Rubin, 1990, call 'naive imputation' – a term aptly reflecting how they feel about this procedure) leads to a situation in which more cases obtain the mean score than would normally be the case: the mean value will be overrepresented in the post-imputation sample, as it is unlikely that all missing values were actually equal to the sample mean. This results in an underestimation of the standard deviation and deflated significance levels (that is, the null hypothesis that there is no effect will be rejected too often: in a multivariate context, the true significance level may be as high as 50 per cent instead of the commonly used 5 per cent).

For all-purpose use, methods that impute a *value* from the predictive distribution rather than a *mean* must be preferred. One example is *stochastic regression imputation*. This is a slight variation on regression imputation, in that the missing x_{i2} is not replaced by its prediction $\hat{x}_{i2}$, as computed using equation 2.3. Instead, equation 2.4 is used:

$$\hat{x}_{i2} = a + b_1 X_1 + r_i, \qquad (2.4)$$

with r_i representing the regression residual from a randomly selected complete case. This method is better for estimating variances and covariances than the various forms of mean imputation, but standard error estimates remain too optimistic. The *multiple imputation* method proposed by Little and Rubin (1990) does not suffer from these drawbacks. The general idea behind this approach is that one does not impute a single value for any particular missing value, but n values ($n > 1$). The imputed values for missing values on variable X_2 could for example be the predicted mean from the regression of variable X_2 on X_1, and $r_{i1}, \ldots, r_{in}$ are randomly drawn residuals from the complete cases, as in stochastic regression imputation. The n values are successively used to create n complete data sets. These n data sets are then analyzed using standard techniques. The n complete-data analyses are then combined, resulting in a single estimate for the parameter of interest. The mean of variable X would for example be the mean of the n means obtained for the n complete-data sets. This method is not very difficult to apply (it is available in the BMDP software package), and performs considerably better than other imputation methods.

All forms of imputation addressed here assume that the missings are MAR. That is, the missingness of a particular variable Y may depend on other (fully observed) variables, but not on values of Y (e.g., if Y is depression and if depressive participants are more likely to drop out, the missing values are not MAR). Thus, unless the MAR assumption can be maintained (which may be hard to ascertain), any form of imputation is likely to lead to erroneous inferences.

A second drawback of imputation methods is that they are only suitable for the treatment of *item* nonresponse – that is, a situation in which a particular case has missing values on one or several variables. Such patterns of missing values diverge strongly from the nonresponse patterns typically found in panel studies. Here the missing data patterns are often *monotone*. In the case of item nonresponse, the missing values are more or less randomly distributed across items and respondents. In panel studies, however, the missings are found for a subsample of participants only, and are cumulative in the sense that once a particular respondent has dropped out, no valid scores will be present in the data matrix. The more credible imputation methods base their estimate of the value to be imputed on the

Table 2.2   *Response probabilities and weights (response probabilities .50 for males and .75 for females, respectively)*

Gender	Wave 1		Wave 2		Weight
	Group size	Proportion	Group size	Proportion	
Males	200	.5	100	.4	1.25
Females	200	.5	150	.6	.83
Total	400	1.0	250	1.0	

scores on other variables that are available for a particular respondent (e.g., stochastic regression imputation and multiple imputation). However, if the values on these other variables are missing as well (as is the case for monotone nonresponse), it becomes difficult to put much faith in the application of these methods, especially if more than a single value is imputed.

Weighting methods discard the incomplete cases and assign new weights to the complete cases, in order to compensate for the dropped cases. These weights are used in subsequent analyses. The most common application of weighting is to unit nonresponse in surveys. The weights are then proportional to the inverse of the response rates of particular groups of respondents. For example, suppose that a sample to be followed through time consists of equal numbers of males and females, at least at the first wave of the study. However, the nonresponse at wave two was selective, and completely accounted for by gender (that is, MAR); males were more likely to drop out of the study than females. This is illustrated in Table 2.2. The response rates were .5 for males and .75 for females, respectively. This resulted in an overrepresentation of the females (who comprise 60 per cent of the sample at wave 2) and, conversely, in an underrepresentation of the males (comprising only 40 per cent of the sample). The weight for the males is then computed as .5 (proportion in the target population) divided by .4 (proportion in the Time 2 sample) equals 1.25, and the weight for the females is computed accordingly. Each observation is then weighted by its appropriate weight. It is also possible to create combinations of variables, e.g., gender, age and socio-economic class, and compute weights for each cell of the resulting three-way table. Another simple and well-used form of weighting is *complete-case analysis*, where the complete cases all receive a weight of 1, and all incomplete cases are discarded (that is, obtain a zero weight). This strategy is also called *listwise deletion of missing values*, which is often the default option when data with missing values are analyzed using a standard statistical package.

Weighting procedures assume that, within a particular stratum (such as gender, age, etc.), respondents and drop-outs have the same (multivariate) distribution on target variables. That is, nonresponders should be a random subsample of the original sample within a particular stratum (thus, their missingness should be MAR). If this assumption is valid, nonresponders can without bias be 'replaced' by responders belonging to the same group. However, the assumption of MAR may be untenable (Waterton and Lievesley, 1987); if so, estimates of means, variances and covariances may be badly biased.

Direct analysis of the incomplete data. The missing data may also be left as gaps in the data set, and the treatment of these is postponed to the analysis phase. Given an incomplete data set, most statistical packages either drop incomplete observations from the sample (this is denoted as *listwise deletion of missing values*; it leaves us with complete-case analysis; see above) or restrict the attention to cases in which the variables of interest are observed (*available-case analysis*).

In available-case analysis, the missing components in the data are replaced by quantities calculable from the available data. For example, univariate statistics (means and standard deviations) are computed using the set of observations for which this variable has been observed, and correlations and covariances are computed on the basis of all pairs of observations for which both variables were observed. This is also called *pairwise deletion of missing values*. The virtues of this approach are its simplicity, and the fact that all available information is used. However, it does not constitute a reliable general approach. Although it is good for estimating distributions (means and standard deviations) because it uses the full sample, it yields biased estimates of other parameters. In some cases, it results in even more bias than complete-case analysis (Little and Rubin, 1990). Furthermore, both listwise and pairwise deletion of missing values assume that the missing values are MCAR – a strong assumption, especially in longitudinal research where drop-out is often not random (as evidenced by the body of research on responder–nonresponder differences; compare the first section of this chapter).

Table 2.3 summarizes the most important features of the methods for handling missing data addressed above. Generally, the methods that can be applied easily either make strong assumptions on the process that generated the missing data (missingness must be MCAR for available-case analysis and complete-case analysis), or they are inappropriate for computing variances and covariances (unconditional and conditional mean imputation). Thus, none of these simple methods is recommended for use in longitudinal data sets.

The other three methods can quite well be applied to longitudinal data sets. In principle, weighting the data is a relatively simple (but often quite effective) strategy. Multiple imputation and stochastic regression imputation are mathematically more sophisticated and perform at least as well as (and often better than) weighting methods, at the cost, however, of ease of use. Further, whereas weighting methods are appropriate for handling unit nonresponse, the other two methods are especially suited to dealing with

Table 2.3   *Comparison of methods for handling missing data*

Method	Virtues	Drawbacks	Assumption
Unconditional mean imputation	Easy to apply	Underestimates standard deviations/errors, and deflated significance levels	MAR
Conditional mean imputation	Easy to apply	Underestimates standard deviations/errors, and deflated significance levels	MAR[1]
Stochastic regression imputation	Prediction across time possible	Difficult to apply	MAR[1]
Multiple imputation	Prediction across time possible, uses all available information	Difficult to apply	MAR[1]
Weighting methods	Well-suited for longitudinal data, relatively easy	Usually a limited number of variables can be involved in computing weights	MAR[1]
Complete-case analysis	Suitable for longitudinal data, easy to apply	Discards all cases with missing data	MCAR[2]
Available-case analysis	Suitable for longitudinal data, uses all available information, easy to apply	May lead to anomalies in the variance/covariance matrix	MCAR[2]

[1] Missing values are missing at random
[2] Missing values are missing completely at random

item nonresponse. All in all, it seems that reweighting the data is the choice to be preferred in compensating the bias that may result from selective nonresponse, especially if a fair amount of the variance in the nonresponse is accounted for by other variables in the data set.

All three methods (weighting methods, stochastic regression imputation, and multiple imputation) assume that the missing data are missing at random. If investigators worry that the missing data are not MAR, one may first analyze the data under the assumption that the missing data are MAR, and then assuming that the missing data are not MAR. Comparison of the results exposes the sensitivity of these to the missing data mechanism. A simple method for deriving the non-MAR results is to distort systematically the imputations from the MAR model. For example, if one is concerned that the missing values for Y are systematically higher than the values that were imputed (as might be the case in income nonresponse), all imputed values for Y might be increased by some plausible amount (say, 20 per cent). If the results based on the distorted data set diverge strongly from those obtained for the original (imputed) data set, there is reason to assume that the missing data were not MAR.

This discussion of methods for handling nonresponse in general and attrition in longitudinal studies in particular shows that there is no single method that is both easy-to-apply and effective. Weighting the complete cases is the first choice to deal with possible bias caused by non-random drop-out, but this procedure relies on the untestable and often implausible assumption that the nonresponders are more or less similar to those who remained in the study. As Kalton and Kasprzyk (1986: 14) note, '. . . *all* methods of handling missing survey data must depend on untestable assumptions. If the assumptions are seriously in error, the analyses may give misleading conclusions. The *only* secure safeguard against serious nonresponse bias in survey estimates is to keep the amount of missing data small' (my italics). This message is also acknowledged by Little and Rubin (1990) and other authors: it is better to be safe, than to be sorry afterwards.

Summary

This chapter discussed the occurrence, detection, implications and treatment of missing values, (unit) nonresponse and drop-out in longitudinal survey research. Drop-out and unit nonresponse can probably never be avoided completely. It is therefore important that an investigator gains insight into the degree to which nonresponse and drop-out were selective, and which factors account for the nonresponse. Such knowledge may also be of use when adjusting for the sample bias that may result when nonresponse is selective. Unfortunately, all methods designed to correct for selective nonresponse ultimately rest on untestable assumptions. Thus, the best way of handling missing data and drop-out is to make sure that there is none. While acknowledging that this cannot be achieved, researchers should take every conceivable measure to optimize their response rates. Only then can they be reasonably certain that the possible bias due to selective nonresponse is as small as possible.

Further reading

The issues discussed in this chapter have generated a large and still growing body of research. Dillman's (1978) text on his Total Design Method is still a very useful text in the field of designing mail and telephone surveys, providing many useful hints on collecting survey data. Since Dillman wrote his classic textbook, computer-assisted telephone interviewing has become enormously popular. Saris (1991) addresses this issue more fully, and his book can be read as an appendix to Dillman (1978).

Goyder (1987) provides an extensive discussion of nonresponse in various types of research, including many suggestions on nonresponse prevention. As regards methods for dealing with nonresponse, Little and Rubin (1987) provide an elaborate and mathematically sophisticated general introduction to the analysis of missing values. Their book does not address nonresponse (attrition) in a longitudinal context, but extensions to longitudinal designs can be found in Little (1995) and Engel and Reinecke (1994).

[ex] effect of children on
quality of marriage
what determines quality? —
young (material)
- vacations per year
- neighborhood or house size
old (spiritual)
- helping others
- closeness to God

researcher does not want to look at the kind of
quality to change, but rather the amount
(qualitative)   (quantitative)
normative   level
ie, the structure has been maintained

3 Measuring Concepts across Time: Issues of Stability and Meaning

This chapter addresses the concept of change (and its complement, stability) in longitudinal research. I first discuss four types of across-time change that may occur (structural, normative, level, and ipsative stability, respectively), showing that the latter three types of change (stability) can only be examined if the structure of a concept that has repeatedly been measured did not change across time. Then a three-step confirmatory factor-analytic procedure is presented to examine various types of across-time change in the structure and meaning of concepts. Finally, an example of this procedure is presented.

What do we talk about when we talk about stability and change?

Most – if not all – longitudinal survey research focuses on change and its prediction. Across-time change is often examined in terms of mean differences on data collected at the waves of the study. For example, are married couples right in thinking that having children will improve the quality of their marriage (Glenn and McLanahan, 1982)? How does the transition toward non-virginhood affect the sexual behavior and sexual attitudes of young people (Taris and Semin, 1995)? How do the perceptions, needs, and personal reactions of newcomers in an organization change as a result of the organizational socialization practices they encounter (Feij et al., 1995)? In cases like these, the longitudinal approach has yielded valuable insights into the effects of events such as childbirth and first sexual intercourse, and organizational socialization practices, on the attitudes and behaviors of people. However, a parallel line of research has demonstrated that phenomenological processes may lead people to constitute and reconstitute their interpretation of their environment and the events that occurred to them (Berger and Luckman, 1966; Gergen, 1977; Mortimer et al., 1982).

Changes in the way people conceptualize variables (that is, reconstitute them) can legitimately be examined in their own right. For example, Schaubroeck and Green (1989) argue that the inevitable surprise and sense making that occur during entry into an organization will lead newcomers in that organization to reinterpret and revise the meaning of concepts such as job satisfaction and organizational commitment. In a somewhat different context, Schaie et al. (1989) focused on the relations among the five primary cognitive abilities (inductive reasoning, spatial orientation, verbal ability, numerical ability, and perceptual speed) across the life-course. By examining the across-age development of intelligence, they essentially examined whether the meaning of this concept changes with age: does intelligence at age 15 refer to the same properties as at age 65?

As these examples show, across-time reconstitutions of variables can be of considerable interest in their own right. However, such reconceptualizations also challenge an investigator's ability to interpret mean differences across time. If the variables of interest are not stable dimensions of reality, testing mean differences across time is complicated, if not impossible. For example, Patterson (1993) argues that the form and definition of antisocial behavior in children alter as the child's age increases. He regards the child's antisocial trait as a *chimera*. According to the ancient Greeks, the chimera was a fire-breathing creature that was part goat, part lion, and part snake. Biologists apply the term for an unusual hybrid produced by grafting tissue from different organisms, a once-popular pastime among Chinese taxidermists trying to fool European mariners (Gould, 1991). According to Patterson (1993), the chimera is an appropriate metaphor for the antisocial trait; each addition of a qualitatively new behavioral problem, and each change in the form of the antisocial behavior, may be thought of as a graft made onto the original trait score. If such changes occur, how can it be said that researchers are examining the same thing across time?

Indeed, even if investigators are not interested in across-time reconceptualizations of variables per se, they must at least *check* whether the variables of interest really represent stable dimensions of reality. To this aim, this chapter first presents a discussion of various types of across-time change that may occur. I then describe a procedure that allows for a systematic test of whether particular types of change have occurred.

Types of change and stability

Mortimer et al. (1982) distinguished among four types of across-time stability. *Structural invariance* refers to the degree of continuity in the nature of a phenomenon under investigation. For example, a personality construct may be considered structurally invariant when it is characterized by the same dimensions, and when there is a persistent pattern of relationships among its component attributes across time (Mortimer et al., 1982). This issue has received much interest in developmental psychology (especially in relation to

similar factor loadings

the across-time development of cognitive abilities, Schaie et al., 1989), but it is highly relevant to other disciplines as well. The generally accepted criterion for structural invariance is that the factor structure of the concept of interest is the same at each wave of the study. Thus, if a particular concept consists of two related factors at one occasion with three items loading on each factor, a similar structure should be obtained for follow-up measurements of this concept. If not, development has been *discontinuous* (other authors have used the terms 'structural', 'qualitative', or 'configural' change when referring to this issue, Baltes and Nesselroade, 1973; Gergen, 1977; Schaie et al., 1989).

Normative stability refers to the persistence of individual ranks or differences on an attribute of interest (Kagan, 1980). It is usually measured as the correlation between the measures of this attribute across time for a group of individuals (such correlations are sometimes referred to as 'autocorrelations'). Strong positive autocorrelations indicate that persons who received low (high) scores in relation to the other members of this group at one wave of a study retained similar relative positions in a follow-up wave. Conversely, weak autocorrelations suggest that the relative position of the persons in the study has changed strongly across time. Please note that it is only meaningful to compare individual ranks on an attribute of interest across time if the meaning of this attribute has remained unchanged. So in order to be able to say that a concept is normatively stable, the assumption that this is structurally invariant must be satisfied. Thus, a prudent investigator will first examine the structural invariance of the concept of interest across time before turning to the issue of normative stability.

Ipsative stability can be defined in terms of 'intraindividual consistencies and change in the organization of attributes over time' (Emmerich, 1968: 671). It refers to the within-person ordering of attributes or the relative strength of behavioral dispositions across time. It is assessed by computing a rank-order correlation coefficient of attributes at two times for each individual respondent. For example, one might examine the stability of a child's preference for several brands of peanut butter, or the salience to the self of particular characteristics such as intelligence, morality, and athletic abilities. In an interesting study, Helwig and Myrin (1997) examined the stability of vocational interests across three generations of one family over a 10-year time span. They found high ipsative stability, and suggested that the gradual changes in vocational preferences over three generations reflected the movement of this family from a rural, farm background to a suburban setting.

Finally, *level stability* (or 'quantitative' stability, Baltes and Nesselroade, 1973) refers to persistence in the magnitude or quantity of a phenomenon across time. Level stability can be measured in terms of (the absence of) change in group means across occasions, such as when there is no

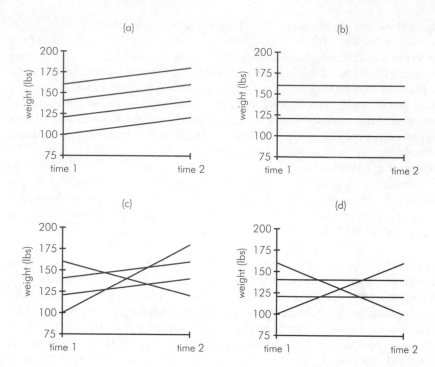

Figure 3.1   *Different combinations of normative and level stability: (a) low
level stability, high normative stability; (b) high level stability, high normative
stability; (c) low level stability, low normative stability; (d) high level stability,
low normative stability*

change in average height in a group of adults. Level stability can also be
assessed at the individual level, by examining within-subject across-time
scores on, say, an IQ-test. Like normative stability, the examination of
level stability presumes that the concepts to be compared are structurally
invariant across time.

Of these four basic types of stability, structural invariance, level stability
and normative stability are frequently addressed in longitudinal survey
research; research questions dealing with ipsative stability seem less preva-
lent, at least in the social and behavioral sciences. Further, it is important to
note that these types of change and stability can occur independently from
each other. For example, consider Figure 3.1. This figure presents four
hypothetical situations. In (a), all persons gain a similar amount of weight
across time, resulting in high normative stability (the correlation between
the two time points is 1.00), whereas level stability is low (their average
weight increases from 130 to 140 pounds). The persons in (c) experience a
similar average increase in weight, but here the correlation between the time
points is $-.80$ (low normative stability; the relative ordering of persons

changes strongly). In (d) we find low normative stability (the across-time correlation equals −.80) coinciding with high level stability (the average weight is 130 pounds at both time points). In (b) there is both high normative and level stability. Clearly, normative and level stability refer to concepts that are not necessarily related. The same applies to the other conceptualizations of stability; these need not occur simultaneously.

Alpha, beta and gamma change. As argued above, examination of normative and level stability is hazardous unless it has been shown that the structure of a particular multi-item concept did not alter across time. The issue of across-time stability has often been addressed in terms of a set of concepts coined by Golembiewski et al. (1976) in an award-winning paper on change and persistence in organizational development designs. They distinguished among three types of across-time change. The first of these is *alpha change*, involving '. . . a variation in the level of some existential state, given a constantly calibrated measuring instrument related to a constant conceptual domain' (1976: 134). Alpha change is simply the opposite of what was heretofore called level stability. What is new is the reference to a 'constantly calibrated measuring instrument'. For instance, when you step on a balance you are probably interested in knowing whether you had gained or lost weight, compared with the preceding measurement of your weight. The measurement of change occurs within a fixed system of stable dimensions of reality (the concept of 'weight'), as defined by an indicator whose intervals are more or less constant (the calibrated marks on the scale of the balance). Now imagine that the intervals between the marks on the scale of this balance are subject to across-time change. In that case it would be impossible to know whether you had gained or lost weight. Golembiewski et al. refer to such phenomena as the result of *beta change*. This is defined as '. . . a variation in the level of some existential state, complicated by the fact that some intervals of the measurement continuum associated with a constant conceptual domain have been recalibrated' (1976: 134).

Beta change with regard to the scale of a balance is unlikely, but the scales of the 'balances' used in the social and behavioral sciences (that is, our items and scales) can certainly be subject to beta change. As argued above, people can constitute and re-constitute their interpretation of a situation through phenomenological processes. You may judge the performance of your car differently after having driven it for two days than after two years, and a couple in marital therapy may evaluate each other differently after a session or two, even if nothing has actually changed. One could say that in all instances of beta change, a change in perspective of the respondents is involved. Respondents may make a different estimate of reality, given a clearer (or just a different) perception of what is the case, or they may highlight different aspects of this reality, due to increased experience or maturational processes. These are common processes in

Table 3.1   *Similarities and differences between the concepts used by Golembiewski et al. (1976) and Mortimer et al. (1982)*

Concepts used by Mortimer et al. (1976)	Concepts used by Golembiewski et al. (1976)	Statistical techniques associated with these concepts
Level stability	Alpha change	T-test, (M)ANOVA
Normative stability	–	Across-time correlations
Structural invariance	Beta + gamma change	Factor analysis
Ipsative stability	–	Within-person correlations

everyday reality, meaning that in longitudinal research there is usually at least the potential for the occurrence of beta change.

The third concept coined by Golembiewski et al. is that of *gamma change*. This involves '. . . a redefinition or reconceptualization of some domain, a major change in the perspective or frame of reference within which phenomena are perceived and classified, in what is taken to be relevant in some slice of reality' (1976: 135). Contrary to beta change, which refers only to variation in the intervals measuring a relatively stable dimension of reality, gamma change is 'big bang' change, a quantum shift in the conceptualization of dimensions of reality. In this respect, the concept of gamma change resembles that of (lack of) structural invariance, the difference being that both beta and gamma change result in a lack of structural invariance. Table 3.1 summarizes the differences between and similarities in Golembiewski et al.'s (1976) and Mortimer et al.'s (1982) approaches. As Table 3.1 shows, Golembiewski et al.'s alpha change can be defined as the absence of Mortimer et al.'s level stability (which is typically assessed though *T*-tests and analysis of variance). Mortimer et al.'s structural invariance comprises Golembiewski et al.'s beta and gamma change. In Golembiewski et al.'s typology there is no counterpart for Mortimer et al.'s normative and ipsative stability.

Golembiewski et al. (1976) not only coined the concepts of alpha, beta, and gamma change. They also proposed that these types of change be examined by means of factor-analytic techniques. By doing so they laid the foundation for a significant body of methods to examine across-time change in the structure and meaning of multi-item concepts. Recently, this literature has exclusively relied on confirmatory factor analysis (CFA; among others Millsap, 1991; Millsap and Hartog, 1988; Pentz and Chou, 1994; Schaubroeck and Green, 1989; Schmitt, 1982; Schmitt et al., 1984; Taris, Bok and Meijer, 1998). It is therefore very helpful to have some idea of what CFA actually involves. The next section provides a brief introduction to factor analysis in general, and the confirmatory factor model in particular. It explains what confirmatory factor analysis does, and why it has become so popular. Readers who are already familiar with the principles of confirmatory factor analysis and its use may prefer to skip this section.

Exploratory vs confirmatory factor analysis

Factor analysis refers to a variety of statistical techniques whose objective is to represent a set of observed variables in terms of a smaller number of unobserved (or 'latent') underlying variables (also called *dimensions* or *factors*, Kim and Mueller, 1978a). For example, a questionnaire may include ten items tapping sexual permissiveness. The responses to these items constitute 'observed' variables. A single score representing a person's score on sexual permissiveness would be far more convenient, however. To this aim, we might compute the mean of all ten items measuring sexual permissiveness. One advantage of this procedure is that the data analysis becomes easier because there are fewer variables to analyze; another is that the reliability of the measurements increases (Cronbach, 1984). However, before combining the ten items into a single overall score we must examine whether these indeed all tap sexual permissiveness. Factor analysis can help us here, by providing information about the number of separate factors that are present in the data, which variables belong to a particular factor, and how strongly the variables are affected by (or 'load on') each factor.

Researchers may have little idea about the structure of their data, for instance, when they have just piloted a newly developed scale. Then factor analysis may show how many factors account for the data, and which observed variables belong to a particular factor. In such cases we speak of *exploratory* factor analysis (EFA). At the other extreme, investigators may want to test their a priori assumptions about the structure of their data. For example, Taris et al. (2000) examined the factorial structure of the Maslach Burnout Inventory (the MBI, Maslach and Jackson, 1986). The MBI was designed to measure burnout as three distinct dimensions, namely emotional exhaustion (referring to feelings of being emotionally over-extended and depleted of one's emotional resources), depersonalization (a negative, indifferent, or overly detached attitude to others), and lack of personal accomplishment (a decline of feelings of competence and success-ful achievement in one's work). In line with this conceptualization, Taris et al. expected that three dimensions would account for their data, with a very specific set of items loading on each of these. If factor analysis seeks to confirm such a priori expectations concerning the structure of the data, one speaks of *confirmatory* factor analysis (CFA).

Traditional procedures for conducting factor analysis (e.g., the SPSS-procedure FACTOR) have two disadvantages that abate their value when it comes to conducting CFA. First, whereas such procedures can tell how many factors account for the data, they do not tell us how these factors should be interpreted. We must a posteriori decide about the nature of a particular factor, based on the pattern of loadings of the items on this factor. However, as investigators tend to highlight different aspects of a particular factor solution, they may well disagree about its correct interpretation.

Second, traditional factor procedures do not allow for an extensive and detailed specification of the factor model that one would like to test. That is, all items must load on all factors; the factors are either all correlated (an oblique model) or all uncorrelated (an orthogonal model); and no relations among the errors of the observed variables can be specified (Long, 1983a). These drawbacks may be acceptable when researchers want to explore their data sets, but traditional factor procedures are clearly a poor tool when they want to test explicit ideas about the structure of their data.

These problems were largely overcome when Jöreskog (1967, 1969) developed the confirmatory factor model. The idea behind this approach is that a researcher must a priori specify the relations between the observed variables and the underlying latent factors. To this aim, the confirmatory factor model allows for a detailed specification of the relations among the observed variables (or 'items'), the errors of these, and the latent factors (or 'dimensions'). Further, Jöreskog (and others, such as Bentler, 1990, and Bentler and Bonett, 1980) devised a range of statistical tests that can be used to judge the degree to which a particular factor model accounts for the observed data (that is, the variances and covariances among the items included in the analysis). Furthermore, several models can be compared on the basis of their ability to account for the data (their 'fit'). Finally, it is also possible to examine the fit of a particular model across two or more groups (or time points), constraining the factor model to be equal across groups (time points).

Taken together, Jöreskog's approach is a very powerful and flexible tool for performing various forms of confirmatory factor analysis. Researchers may test their ideas about the structure of their data, compare a range of factor models that may account for the data, test whether a particular factor model generalizes across groups or occasions, etc. This also implies that the Jöreskog approach to conducting CFA is extremely useful for examining the stability of factor structures across time. Below we discuss how CFA can be used to examine whether gamma and/or beta change has occurred.

Using the confirmatory factor-analytic model to assess structural invariance

As noted earlier on, current research on the structural invariance of constructs across time is strongly rooted in the factor-analytic tradition. In this tradition, gamma change is examined in terms of across-time differences in the number of factors that account for the data and in the patterns of factor loadings. Beta change is measured as change in the magnitude of the loadings of the items on the factors, and/or change in the variances and covariances of the latent and observed variables (Schmitt, 1982).

These ideas can aptly be tested within the framework of Jöreskog's confirmatory factor analysis, as this procedure allows for a very precise specification of the relations among the observed variables and underlying dimensions, and because it provides tests for the fit of a particular factor model to the data. That is, investigators can assess which model accounts best for the data at both time points. If the same basic model applies to both occasions, parts of this model (for example, the factor loadings or the factor variances) can be constrained to be equal across time. Comparison of the fit of a particular constrained model to the fit of a similar unconstrained model may then reveal whether the imposed constraint is empirically plausible (that is, whether the constrained part of the model is invariant across time – no gamma and/or beta change has occurred). If the constrained model cannot be maintained, however, gamma and/or beta change may have occurred.

Below I describe in some detail a three-step confirmatory factor-analytic procedure that can be used to examine the invariance of factor structures across time. It is assumed that the items of interest were measured at two distinct time points. The procedure described below can easily be generalized to multi-wave studies, however.

Step 1: testing the equality of variance–covariance matrixes across time   The first step to be taken is to test the equality of the variance–covariance matrixes among the variables of interest for both time points. Note that across-time comparison of the *correlation* matrix would be inappropriate, because beta change may become manifest in across-time differences in factor- and/or item-variances. As the variances of the items in correlation matrixes are always equal to 1.00 (and, thus, equal across time points), the amount of beta change will be underestimated in across-time comparison of correlation matrixes. A significant difference between the time one and time two variance–covariance matrixes signifies that

1   some form of gamma change has occurred; the number of dimensions has changed across time, or the pattern of factor loadings has changed;
2   some form of beta change has taken place: the variances and/or covariances among the latent variables differ across time points, and/or the magnitude of the loadings of the items on the latent variables have changed;
3   the uniquenesses (or errors) of the observed variables differ across time; or
4   some combination of 1–3 has occurred.

If the test statistics indicate that the variance–covariance matrixes do not differ significantly across time, this does not imply that the analysis is done. It would remain interesting to estimate the equal (but unknown) factor pattern, the factor loadings, and so on.

Second step: gamma change　If the previous analysis revealed that across-time differences in factor structure can be expected, we must check whether the same basic factor structure applies to both time points (in terms of the number of factors and the patterns of factor loadings). At both occasions a *simple structure* should be reached. The 'simple structure' is the simplest factor model (that is, the model with the fewest factors) that accounts well for the data; simpler models (with fewer factors) should fit the data significantly worse, while more complex models (with more factors) should not improve significantly upon this model. Comparison of the fit of various models will usually reveal which of these fits the data best (MacCallum et al., 1992). Further, if the number of factors in the simple structures is the same across time, it must be ascertained that the pattern of factor loadings did not change. That is, the same set of items must load on the same underlying factor at both occasions.

Third step: beta change – testing the equality of factor variances/covariances and scaling units　If the same basic factor structure applies to both time points the issue of beta change can be examined. To test whether beta change has occurred, the loadings of the items on the underlying dimensions must be constrained to be equal across time points. Comparison of the fit indexes obtained for the constrained model to those obtained for the unconstrained model may indicate that the fit of the constrained model is not significantly worse (in which case the factor loadings can be assumed to be equal). Alternatively, the constrained model may fit the data significantly less well than the unconstrained model (in which some form of beta change has occurred).

　　If the assumption of equality of factor loadings across time can be retained, we must examine the equality of the variances and covariances among the latent factors across time. This test focuses on the extent to which respondents see greater integration or differentiation of constructs from one time point to the other. First the covariances among factors within one time point must be set equal to the corresponding covariances among the same factors for the other time point. Successive changes in factor variance across time can be tested using the same procedure.

Example: loneliness across young adulthood

De Jong-Gierveld defined loneliness as '. . . a situation experienced by the participant as one where there is an unpleasant or inadmissible lack of (the quality of) certain social relationships' (1987: 120). In accordance with this notion, De Jong-Gierveld and Kamphuis (1985) developed a two-dimensional 11-item scale to measure loneliness. One scale focuses on feelings of deprivation, with typical items such as 'I feel that my circle of friends and acquaintances is too limited', 'I lack a real good friend'; the other taps feelings of belongingness, with items such as 'There is always someone around that I can talk to about my day to day problems' (reversed), and 'I can always call on my friends whenever I feel like it' (reversed, 1 = 'yes', 3 = 'no'). The scale was used in a panel study among 1,257 young adults (evenly divided across gender and three birth cohorts, namely 1961, 1965 and 1969, respectively). The two waves of the study were conducted in 1987 and 1991. One interesting research question focuses on the development of loneliness across young adulthood. However, in order to provide a valid answer to these questions, it must be shown that the meaning of loneliness is the same across different phases of young adulthood. To this aim, it must be shown that the structure of loneliness is invariant across time (age).

First step: equality of the variance–covariance matrix across time The first step to be taken involves a comparison of the variance–covariance matrixes obtained at the two waves of the study. We must examine whether it can reasonably be assumed that the variances and covariances obtained at one point in time are equal to those obtained at the other time point. At this point, it is convenient to analyze the data matrixes obtained for the two time points as if these were collected from two statistically independent samples. The two 11 × 11 variance–covariance matrixes (one for each time point) were constrained to be equal to each other. The assumption that both matrixes are equal was rejected; chi-square with 66 *df* was 720.92, RMR = .10, NNFI = .81, CFI = .88. Thus, there is reason to assume that some form of gamma and/or beta change occurred.

Second step: gamma change The aim of this step is to see which factor model accounts best for the data obtained at each time point. The data matrixes obtained at each time point are still analyzed separately. As Table 3.2 shows, a one-factor model in which all 11 loneliness-items loaded on the same underlying dimension did not fit the data well. Thus, this model

Table 3.2 *Comparison of the fit of various models, for time 1 and time 2 separately*

Model		χ^2	df	RMR	NNFI	CFI
One-factor model	time 1	711.63	44	.08	.67	.74
	time 2	714.46		.08	.68	.74
Two-factor model	time 1	278.17	43	.05	.88	.91
	time 2	246.91		.04	.90	.92

N.B. RMR = Root Mean Square Residual; NNFI = Non-Formed Fit Index; CFI = Comparative Fit Index

was rejected. A two-dimensional model in which the six 'deprivation' items loaded on one dimension and the six 'belongingness' items on the other, and where the two underlying dimensions were allowed to correlate, fitted the data quite well at both occasions. Thus, it seems that the same factor structure (in terms of the pattern of effects) applied to both time points, suggesting that no gamma change occurred.

Third step: beta change   The full 22×22 variance–covariance matrix must be analyzed in order to examine whether beta change occurred. We first created a longitudinal analog of the 'simple structure' obtained in step 2. The 22 items were assumed to load on one of four underlying dimensions ('deprivation' and 'belongingness', both measured at time 1 and time 2). The 'deprivation' and the 'belongingness'-dimension were allowed to correlate within time points. Further, two autocorrelations were included, between time 1 and time 2 Deprivation, and time 1 and time 2 Belongingness, respectively (note that the magnitude of these autocorrelations signifies the degree to which there is normative stability across time). Apart from the basic factor structure for loneliness (in terms of two underlying dimensions, each corresponding with a particular set of items), this model does not contain any across-time constraints. This model (M_1) served as a baseline model against which the fit of other models (incorporating across-time constraints on the magnitude of the loadings, factor covariances, and factor variances, respectively) could be compared.

M_1 fitted the data reasonably well: NNFI = .89, CFI = .91 (see Table 3.3; according to Bentler and Bonett, 1980, an NNFI of .90 or over indicates a good fit). Then the loadings of the factors were constrained to be equal across time (model M_2). This resulted in a gain of 9 *df* at a loss of 30.64 chi-square points. Although M_2 fitted the data significantly less well than M_1, the NNFI and CFI remained unchanged. Thus, whereas there were statistically significant differences in the factor loadings obtained for each time point, these do not seem very large. In a third model (M_3) the covariance between the two dimensions of loneliness was constrained to be equal across time. The 2.88 increase in chi-square at a gain of 1 *df* is not significant. Thus, the participants did not see greater or lesser integration

Table 3.3   *Invariance across time of various models for loneliness*

Model	χ_2	df	RMR	NNFI	CFI
M_1 longitudinal	999.96	205	.06	.89	.91
M_2 loadings equal	1030.60	214	.07	.89	.91
M_3 covars equal	1033.48	215	.07	.89	.91
M_4 vars equal	1069.34	217	.07	.88	.89

of these two dimensions of loneliness. Then the variances of the underlying dimensions were constrained across time (model M_4). This resulted in a gain of 2 *df* at a loss of no less than 35.86 chi-square points. Despite this significant detorioration of the fit of this model, NNFI and CFI remained quite acceptable.

Figure 3.2 presents the results obtained for model M_3. Here the factor loadings (constrained across occasions) are given, as are the autocorrelations and the proportion of explained variance in the items. All estimates are expressed in a common metric, and can readily be compared across time. As Figure 3.2 shows, the basic structure of the model is identical for both occasions. The number of factors is the same, as are the patterns of factor loadings. Thus, no gamma change has occurred.

Figure 3.2 shows that the factor loadings are generally quite low. This results in rather low proportions of explained variances among the items. Further, the proportions of explained variance vary across time: an additional analysis in which these were constrained to be equal resulted in an increase of about 500 chi-square points with a gain of only 11 *df*. Generally, the *R*-squares are higher at the second wave of the study, suggesting that the current conceptualization of loneliness fitted the time 2 data somewhat better than the time 1 data. The correlation between the two dimensions of loneliness is moderately high (.41, $p < .001$), and the same for both occasions. Finally, the autocorrelations presented in Figure 3.2 show that being lonely is not a very stable phenomenon. For the 'belongingness' dimension we found an across-time correlation coefficient of .45 (which is low, given the one-year interval between the waves of the study; autocorrelations in the range .60–.80 are quite common for such time intervals). The stability of the 'deprivation'-dimension is even lower (.19). Clearly, the normative stability of loneliness is low.

Given these results, we may conclude that (a) the basic factor structure of loneliness did not change across time (no gamma change); (b) there is some evidence that beta change has occurred, given that the model accounted better for the time 2 data than for the time 1 data, the across-time differences in the variances of the latent dimensions, and the differences in the proportions of explained variance; (c) the normative stability of the two dimensions of loneliness is quite low, at least among young adults.

Discussion

This chapter addressed the issues of change and stability of concepts. I distinguished among several forms of across-time change, and showed how several of these can be examined using confirmatory factor analysis. I mainly focused on structural invariance, as the examination of other forms

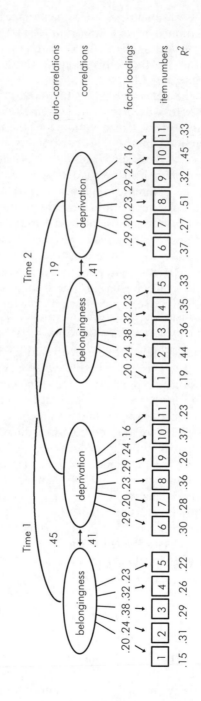

Figure 3.2 Results of an analysis of the invariance of a two-factor model (M_3) across time

of change implies that the structure of the concept of interest has remained invariant across time. In my opinion, as yet this issue has not fully been appreciated. Textbooks addressing longitudinal research almost never discuss the issue of the structural invariance at any length, and it is interesting – if not disquieting – to note that papers reporting the results of longitudinal studies seldom mention that the structural invariance of the concepts in the study has been checked. The take-home message will be clear: I firmly believe that researchers should check the across-time validity of their measures, preferably using state-of-the-art methodology: Why run the risk of drawing incorrect conclusions about what is the case in the data, if there are methods available that can rule out alternative explanations for a particular set of results? This applies even more to longitudinal survey research, precisely because designing and doing such a study requires so much effort – why waste all the time, care, and effort spent on collecting the data by doing sloppy data analysis?

Further reading

A seminal paper on the issue of structural invariance of concepts in longitudinal research is that by Golembiewski et al. (1976), which focuses on conceptual rather than technical matters, and provides several real-life examples taken from work and industrial psychology. They also coined the terminology used throughout this chapter. Mortimer et al. (1982) discuss four types of change (including structural change), and show that these do not necessarily lead to similar results. Kim and Mueller (1978a, 1978b) present a perhaps somewhat dated (but still very useful) introduction to exploratory factor analysis. Jöreskog (1979a, 1979b), Pentz and Chou (1994), Schmitt (1982), and Schaubroeck and Green (1989), present introductions in how to use confirmatory factor-analytic techniques to assess structural invariance in longitudinal research. Introductions to confirmatory modeling in general can be found in Hayduk (1989), Loehlin (1998), and Long (1983a, 1983b); Bollen (1989) presents a comprehensive, although mathematically rather more sophisticated, review of the confirmatory model.

4   Issues in Discrete-time Panel Analysis

This chapter deals with the analysis of change when the data are collected at discrete time points (as in a panel study). There are several important problems that impede straightforward analysis and interpretation of apparent across-wave change. One of these is the presumed unreliability of change scores. The across-time difference between two measures of a particular variable is a natural measure of the amount of change that has occurred. Yet, this type of analysis has become notorious – but is this justified, and what are possible alternatives? Another issue is the dependence of the amount of change on 'initial values' – that is, on the score obtained at the first wave of the study; one example of this phenomenon is regression toward the mean. Finally, a method for assessing causal priority using two or more measurements of a pair of variables is addressed (*cross-lagged panel analysis*).

Measuring change in discrete time

Whereas the previous chapter dealt with the across-time structural invariance of a particular concept, this chapter discusses the analysis of other types of across-time change. In doing so, it is assumed that the structure of the concept of interest is invariant across time. A further assumption is that the data were collected at discrete points in time – that is, the scores of the participants on the variables of interest are assumed to be known at the waves of the study only. Although this may seem trivial, information on the participants' scores between the waves can be obtained by asking retrospective questions (for example, 'you just said that you and your partner broke up since the last interview. Can you tell me the month and year when you broke up?'). The first chapter in this volume dealt more extensively with the issue of retrospective questions, whereas Chapter 6 provides a more elaborate discussion of discrete versus continuous time data.

Figure 4.1 gives a schematic representation of a three-wave discrete-time panel study. At each wave of the study, information is collected on the attitudes, behaviors and the like of the participants; no information is available prior to the first wave, after the third wave, or in between the waves. Thus, the data set contains three 'snapshots' of each participant in

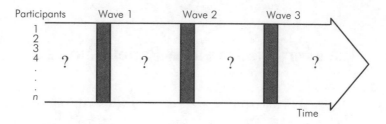

Figure 4.1   *Three-wave panel study, discrete-time data*

the study; the intervals between the waves and before the first wave of the study are white boxes. Note, however, that even this rather simple research design may well provide some information about what happened to the participants between the waves. For instance, if a particular participant held one job at the first wave of the study and another at the second, it is obvious that this person has found a different job elsewhere.

If we *do* have information about the intervals between the waves of a particular longitudinal study, we speak of *continuous-time data*. Chapter 6 discusses this issue more fully in the context of discrete-time versus continuous-time survival analysis. The current chapter, however, only deals with discrete-time information and methods appropriate for analyzing this particular data type.

Dependence on initial values: the sophomore slump

It has often been noted that the amount and direction of across-time change tends to depend to a considerable degree on the initial score of the participant. One typical example is James Wilder's 'law of initial values' (Wilder, 1967). He described his 'law' (which was based on experience, and not intended as a description of what will always and necessarily be the case) as follows:

> Given a standard stimulus and a standard period of time, the extent and direc-
> tion of response of a psychophysiological function at rest depends to a large
> measure on its initial (pre-experimental) level. The relations are as follows: The
> higher the initial value, the smaller the response to function raising, the larger the
> response to function-depressing stimuli. Beyond a certain medium range of initial
> values there is a tendency to paradoxic (reversed) responses, increasing with the
> extremeness of initial values. (Wilder, 1967: viii)

Thus, Wilder argues that participants who obtained a very high (low) score on a particular variable will usually show little response to a stimulus meant to increase (decrease) their score on this variable. This principle also generalizes to nonexperimental contexts. For example, if workers are already intensely satisfied with their jobs (as reflected in, say, an average score of 6.5 on a seven-point satisfaction scale), measures intended to raise their job satisfaction will usually have little effect (this is called a _ceiling effect;_ the reverse effect – having an extremely low score that can hardly become lower, whatever happens – is called a _floor_ effect). On the other hand, people who obtained an extremely high (low) score will react forcefully to measures intended to _decrease_ (increase) their score on this variable. Lord (1963: 22) gives the example of weight loss. People are weighed at two points in time: those who lost much weight at time 2 will usually have been quite corpulent at time 1; conversely, extreme gainers can be expected to have been quite thin.

Wilder (1967) states that beyond a 'certain medium range' of initial values, responses tend to be the reverse of what one would expect: extremely low initial scores will be followed by an increase at a follow-up study, while extremely high initial scores tend to be followed by lower follow-up scores. This phenomenon is usually denoted as the _regression effect_ or _regression toward the mean_ (Thorndike, 1924). Regression toward the mean is often framed in terms of measurement error (Hsu, 1995; Speer, 1992). That is, the score on a particular measuring instrument may not only reflect a participant's 'true' score on the underlying concept, but may have been influenced by other factors as well. For example, Taylor and Cuave (1995) examined the 'sophomore slump' among professional baseball players. This term refers to a significant decline in competitive performance during an athlete's second (or sophomore) year at a given level of competition following an outstanding first (or rookie) season. Such a decline may be due to the changes which accompany outstanding play in a rookie year; these may produce significant stress for the athlete, that could adversely affect performance during the sophomore season (for example, greater time demands may limit off-season physical and technical development, and greater expectations may generate self-doubt about one's own ability to live up to these expectations). Alternatively, the 'sophomore slump' could be the result of regression toward the mean, caused by measurement unreliability. Outstanding performance during the rookie year could be due to incidental factors or mere luck, and not only to the rookie's qualities; if so, outstanding rookie performances are likely to regress toward their actual level of ability.

If the 'stress' interpretation is correct, baseball sophomores can be expected to 'bounce back' to their initial level of performance after their sophomore year, as experienced players will have learnt how to cope with the stress resulting from being a baseball star. However, if the regression to the mean (or measurement unreliability)-interpretation applies, no bouncing back will occur; outstanding performances during their first year are due to random factors which on average helped to increase rookies' performance. Taylor and Cuave collected archival data on the performance of major league baseball hitters who had outstanding rookie seasons. Consistent with the regression to the mean view, they found that the mean batting average of outstanding rookies declined significantly from .300 in their first year, via .276 in their sophomore year, to on average .269 for the third to fifth year of their careers – still quite good, but not spectacularly so. Thus, it seems that outstanding rookie performances are often the result of incidental factors whose favorable effects on performance tend to disappear in time, meaning that the batting average is not a very reliable measure of the true qualities of a sophomore baseball player.

Although this example gives a fair impression of what is meant by regression to the mean, it is desirable to define this phenomenon more formally. Regression to the mean occurs when the mean of all posttest scores x'' following a particular pretest score x', is closer to the posttest mean $E(X'')$ than this particular pretest x' is to the pretest mean $E(X')$ (Rogosa and Willett, 1985: 'E' for 'expected value'). Hence, regression to the mean occurs when the difference between the 'overall' mean at time 2 and the time 2 mean of all participants who have a particular score x' at time 1, is smaller than the difference between the 'overall' mean at time 1 and the time 1 score x' of these participants:

$$|E(X''|X'=x') - E(X'')| < |x'-E(X')|. \qquad (4.1)$$

For instance, assume that the participants in a study completed a seven-point life satisfaction scale at two occasions. Let at both time points the average level of satisfaction be 3.5. Let us now examine the time 2 scores of those who were very satisfied at time 1 (those who obtained a score of, say, 6). The average time 1 score for this group is 6; the difference between the time 1 mean of this group and the 'overall' time 1 mean is (6 minus 3.5 equals) 2.5. If the difference between the time 2 overall mean and the time 2 mean of the group of participants who obtained a score of 6 at time 1 is smaller than 2.5, regression to the mean has occurred. Obviously, this condition is satisfied if the average time 2 score for this group is lower than 6.

It has long been believed impossible to avoid regression toward the mean. For example, Furby (1973: 172) felt that 'Regression toward the mean is *ubiquitous* in developmental psychological research' (my italics). However, it can be shown (Rogosa, 1988; Speer, 1992) that regression toward the mean occurs only when the correlation between the initial score and the amount of across-time change is negative (that is, when ceiling and/or floor effects occur, leading to a decrease of the variance of the participants' scores across time). However, this correlation can well be zero or even positive (if the variance among the scores increases across time; this is known as *fanspread*, Rogosa, 1988). However, regression toward the mean tends to occur most frequently.

Regression to the mean and, more generally, dependence on initial values are often treated as statistical artifacts. That is, no substantive interpretation is necessary to account for these phenomena; they are not considered as theoretically interesting. Indeed, regression to the mean is sometimes 'controlled' by omitting participants with extreme time 1 scores from the sample, thus focusing on the 'certain medium range of initial values' mentioned by Wilder (1967). A possibly more viable procedure is to ensure that ceiling and floor effects will not occur, by constructing variables in such a way that they provide a broader range of categories than will normally be used by the respondents (Kessler, 1977).

Change scores: what is the difference?

The difference between the scores obtained at two time points is a natural estimate of the amount of change from one occasion to another. For example, if the variable of interest is income, then subtracting the income measured at time 1 from the income measured at time 2 represents the income gain (or loss) during the interval between time 1 and time 2. This quantity is usually termed the *difference score* or *change score*. Intuitively attractive as the difference score may seem, its use has generated much concern from statisticians and methodologists. They saw at least two problems. One is the presumed unreliability of difference scores; the other is what has come to be known as the 'regression fallacy'.

Unreliability of difference scores   It has frequently been noted that difference scores are less reliable than the constituent variables (e.g., Burr and Nesselroade, 1990; Cronbach and Furby, 1970; Hsiao, 1986; Kessler, 1977; Kessler and Greenberg, 1981; Lord, 1963; Plewis, 1985). Assume that the reliabilities and variances of two repeated measurements of variable Y (Y_1 and Y_2, respectively) are identical across time. The reliability of the $Y_2 - Y_1$ difference score is then equal to

$$\frac{\rho_Y^2 - \rho_{12}}{1 - \rho_{12}}, \tag{4.2}$$

with ρ_{12} denoting the correlation between Y_1 and Y_2, and ρ_Y^2 their common reliability. If ρ_{12} is positive (as will usually be the case), then the reliability of the difference score must necessarily be lower than the reliability of the constituent variables. Indeed, the higher the correlation between Y_1 and Y_2, the lower the reliability of the difference score will be; as Lord put it, 'the difference between two fallible measures is frequently much more

Table 4.1 *Reliability of difference scores as a function of the reliability of two variables and their correlation*

Reliability of Y_1 and Y_2	Correlation between Y_1 and Y_2			
	.80	.60	.40	.20
.80	.00	.50	.66	.75
.60	–	.00	.33	.50
.40	–	–	.00	.25
.20	–	–	–	.00

fallible than either' (1963: 32). This principle is illustrated in Table 4.1, where the reliability of a difference score is shown for different levels of ρ_Y^2 and ρ_{12}. Table 4.1 reveals that the reliability of the difference score decreases when the correlation between the two constituent variables increases. If the common reliability is .80 and the correlation between the variables is as high as .60, the reliability of the difference score is .50; this increases to a quite acceptable .75 when the correlation between Y_1 and Y_2 decreases to .20. If the reliability of the component variables is only .60, the reliability of the difference score becomes extremely low. For example, if the correlation between Y_1 and Y_2 is .40, the reliability of the corresponding difference score is an alarmingly low .33, suggesting that the participants' scores on this variable are little more than random error.

On second thoughts, however, investigators should not be surprised about the typically low reliability of change scores. As Rogosa (1988) notes, the time 1 minus time 2 true score correlation ξ_{12} (that is, the correlation between Y_1 and Y_2, after correction for measurement error) is large for almost all regions of Table 4.1, as can be seen from the disattenuation formula $\xi_{12} = \rho_{12}/\rho_Y^2$. In particular, ξ_{12} equals 1.00 along the diagonal of zero reliability for the difference score. A high time 1 minus time 2 correlation with equal across-time variances implies that there are almost no individual differences in the amount of true change (if there is any), and the difference score cannot be expected to detect them. Further, if there are almost no individual differences in across-time change, the low reliability of the difference score should come as no surprise.

The fact that the reliability of a difference score tends to be much lower than the reliability of the constituent variables has led researchers to propose several measures. One strategy focuses on the reliability of the constituent variables. As the reliability of difference scores becomes especially problematic if the reliability of the constituent variables is low, one simple solution is to *raise the reliability of these constituent variables* by increasing the number of items measuring a particular concept (Cronbach, 1984: 174), or by replacing bad items with better items (with a view to increase the homogeneity of the scale and, thus, its reliability).

Alternatively, investigators ought to *consider the 'appropriate' time interval between two consecutive waves* of a study, to ensure that true change has taken place (Kessler, 1977). The spacing between the waves of a study should be such that the difference between two consecutive measurements of a variable reflects (at least partly) true change, and not only random across-time fluctuations (note that a longer interval between two measurements of the same variable will usually lead to a lower correlation between these). Although this seems reasonable, the difficulty is to know what the 'appropriate' length of this time interval is. Therefore, this rule of thumb does not offer much help in everyday practice.

The regression fallacy: regression to the mean and difference scores Jennings and Markus (1977) examined the effect of having served in the army on feelings of trust toward the government. They might have done so by comparing army veterans' trust scores to the scores of people without any army experience. The obvious flaw in this design is that these two groups may have differed initially on trust in the government; it is likely that veterans initially put more faith in the government than non-veterans, or else they would not have chosen to join the army (the recruits enlisted voluntarily). Therefore, it is imperative that initial differences in trust be controlled. To this aim, Jennings and Markus conducted a two-wave panel study, the first wave of which was conducted in 1965 (when all respondents were high school seniors), and the second in 1973.

One way of analyzing the data is to compare the time 1 minus time 2 trust difference score of the two groups of interest, controlling their time 1 trust scores. However, this strategy is fraught with difficulties. As discussed earlier on, difference scores tend to be negatively correlated with initial scores: the higher initial trust, the lower the gains will be. If veterans had somewhat higher time 1 trust scores than non-veterans, the former will display relatively smaller gains under the null hypothesis of no effect. If this regression effect is ignored, we might well conclude that military experience had a deleterious effect on trust when, in truth, the null hypothesis is correct (Markus, 1979). This has been termed the *regression fallacy*. Kessler (1977) pointed out that the term 'fallacy' is not altogether correct: assuming that all measurements are perfectly reliable, the phenomenon of regression to the mean actually reflects *true* change. The fallacy occurs only if the regression effects are attributed to the effects of the independent variables in the study (Markus, 1979).

Both issues have led to grave warnings against the use of difference scores. For example, Cronbach and Furby stated in their influential paper that 'There is no need to use measures of change as dependent variables and no virtue in using them' (1970: 78). They recommended that other approaches to analyzing change be used instead of difference scores. One of these is discussed below.

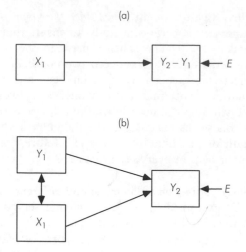

Figure 4.2   *Analysis of change: (a) the difference score approach; (b) the regressor variable approach*

The regressor variable approach, and the return of the difference score

One frequently applied alternative to the use of difference scores is what Allison (1990) called the *regressor variable method*. Assume that variables X and Y have been measured at two consecutive waves of a panel study. Variable X is assumed to affect variable Y. In the difference score approach, the $Y_2 - Y_1$ difference score would be regressed on X_1 (Figure 4.2(a)). In the regressor variable method, Y_2 is regressed on Y_1 and X_1 (Figure 4.2(b)). Thus, the score on Y on the first occasion is treated here like any other explanatory variable.

Hence, instead of trying to explain the difference (thus, the gain or loss) in Y during the observed interval, the regressor variable approach accounts for Y_2 holding Y_1 constant. Stated differently: what predicts change in Y_2, controlling the initial score at T_1? Although this appears to be a rather different research question than the question in the change score approach, it is not: in both approaches the focus is usually on the effects of other variables on the development of Y in time, not on the amount of change in Y itself.

One alternative approach that has been advocated is to regress the difference score $Y_2 - Y_1$ on both Y_1 and other control variables, thus controlling the initial level of Y (thus controlling ceiling and/or floor effects: is it the case that those who obtain an extremely low or high score experience more or less change than those who have a moderately high score at time 1?). As Werts and Linn (1970) showed, regressing the difference score on X_1 and Y_1 yields the same results as regression of Y_2 on Y_1 and X_1. Hence, this is just a slightly more complicated variation on the regressor variable method.

Although there is no obvious drawback to the regressor variable method, since the middle of the 1970s psychometrists' negative attitude towards the use of difference scores has tempered somewhat (Burr and Nesselroade, 1990). There are circumstances under which the reliability of difference scores can be high (Sharma and Gupta, 1986), while difference scores can yield powerful tests of causal hypotheses, in spite of their unreliability (Maxwell and Howard, 1981). Kenny and Cohen (1979) and Allison (1990) argued that regression towards the mean is not a problem when the investigator compares two or more stable groups. Indeed, in such cases the difference score approach may yield results with even less bias than the regressor variable approach. Hence, these authors call for a rehabilitation of the difference score.

Return of the difference score

Allison (1990) formulated conditions under which the difference score approach performs equally well or even better than the regressor variable approach. This is the case in the *non-equivalent control group design* (see Chapters 1 and 5). The participants in a longitudinal study can post-hoc be assigned to a control and a treatment group; the participants in the treatment group experienced a particular event between the waves of the study, the participants in the control group did not. By comparing the scores of the control and the treatment group insight is obtained into the effects of the 'treatment'. The difference between this design and a true experimental design is that in the non-equivalent control group design the participants are *not* randomly assigned to the control and the treatment groups, which implies that these groups may differ substantially regarding their scores on Y_1. The nonequivalent control group design is especially appropriate in the case of surveys, as in this case the treatment is not under the control of the researcher. For example, in studying the effects of a divorce on feelings of loneliness, the sample will post-hoc be divided into a treatment and a control group; it may well be the case that those who are about to experience a divorce differ substantially – both in terms of their feelings of loneliness and of other variables – from the control group.

In the regressor variable approach, a suitable regression model for such data is

$$Y_{i2} = \alpha + \beta_1 Y_{i1} + \beta_2 X_i + \varepsilon_i. \qquad i = 1, \ldots, n \qquad (4.3)$$

That is, the score on variable Y of participant i at time 2 (Y_{i2}) consists of a constant α, an effect of the score of this participant on Y at time 1 (Y_{i1}) weighted by an effect parameter β_1, an effect of a dichotomous variable X_i indicating whether participant i received the treatment ($X_i = 1$) or not ($X_i = 0$) weighted by an effect parameter β_2, and random error in the error term ε_{i1}.

Now define an additional variable G, signifying whether an observation is in the group that receives the treatment. This variable is conceptually different from X, that indicated whether the treatment has actually been received. The distinction between X and G seems somewhat artificial, and indeed, in this context G is identical to X at time 2 (but not at time 1). Allison (1990) then proposes separate equations for Y_1 and Y_2:

$$Y_{i1} = \alpha + \gamma G_i + \varepsilon_{i1}, \qquad i = 1, \ldots, n \qquad (4.4a)$$
$$Y_{i2} = \alpha + \tau + \gamma G_i + \beta_1 X_i + \varepsilon_{i2} \qquad (4.4b)$$

Hence, the score of participant i on variable Y at time 1 is a function of a constant α, a constant group difference γG_i, and some random error in ε_{i1}. At time 2, Y is composed of constant α, constant γG_i, an effect of variable X weighted by effect parameter β_1, some random error in ε_{i2}, and a constant τ that reflects the change over time that applies to all individuals in both the control and treatment group.

Obviously, in equation 4.4b, variables X and G cannot be distinguished from each other, as they are completely collinear (that is, if X is the case, G is also the case, and if X is not present, G is absent as well; there is no observation for which X is the case but to which G does not apply, and vice versa). However, by subtracting 4.4a from 4.4b, we obtain

$$Y_{i2} - Y_{i1} = \tau + \beta_1 X_i + \varepsilon_i^*, \qquad i = 1, \ldots, n \qquad (4.5)$$

with $\varepsilon_i^* = \varepsilon_{i2} - \varepsilon_{i1}$. As both error terms are assumed to contain only random error, the expectation of these error terms is zero. Therefore, the expectation of ε_i^* is zero as well: $E(\varepsilon_{i2}|X_i) - E(\varepsilon_{i1}|X_i) = 0$ for all i. In effect, this justifies the difference score method: equation 4.5 can be estimated without bias.

But what about the unreliability of difference scores? As shown above, one important reason for discouraging using difference scores was their presumed unreliability, at least when the across-time correlation of the measures is high and their reliabilities low. Allison (1990) argues that this is not really a problem. We need not be concerned about unreliability; what matters is the *error variance* in equation 4.5, as this determines the precision of the estimate of β_1. Indeed, it can be shown that the low reliability of difference scores is completely irrelevant for the purpose of causal inference. As Allison aptly put it,

. . . the ideal situation for detecting a treatment effect is one in which the subjects who do not receive the treatment hardly change at all from pre-test to post-test, while the subjects in the treatment group all change by exactly the same amount. But this is just the situation that produces high correlations between pre-test and post-test, and, therefore, low reliability of change scores. The low reliability results from the fact that in calculating the change score we differ out all the stable between-subject variation, except for that due to the treatment effect. (1990: 105)

Hence, it seems that using difference scores in survey research has been discouraged on grounds that were largely irrelevant. Despite the possibly low reliability of difference scores, this approach may yield powerful tests of causal hypotheses; these two issues are largely independent from each other. How should one choose between the difference score approach and the regressor variable approach? Although there are subtle statistical and theoretical considerations that may play a role (see Allison, 1990, for a discussion of these), both approaches will generally do quite a good job in accounting for the typical empirical patterns found in data produced by the nonequivalent control group design.

Example: income determination among men and women

As an illustration of some of the procedures outlined in this chapter, we examine the income development across time of a sample of 389 young Dutch adults at the start of their employment career. The human capital theory assumes that income is determined by productivity: the higher a worker's productivity, the more their employer will be willing to pay them. In turn, productivity is determined by level of education and experience; higher-educated and more-experienced workers should have a higher income than their less-experienced and lower-educated colleagues.

In this approach, education and experience are the main predictors of income. However, one common finding is that women tend to earn less than men. The human capital-framework accounts for this finding by assuming that women invest less in their education than men, as they will expect an interruption of their employment career, as at some time they will have to care for their young children. This means that they expect to have less time to earn back their investment in education than men: thus, for women it is not rational to invest in education (see the famous book on 'household economics' by Nobel prize laureate Gary S. Becker, 1981). However, during the last two or three decades the difference in level of education of men and women has disappeared; yet, gender differences in income continue to exist. The current application examines the across-time relations between pay and level of education, job level, and gender: is it indeed the case that women earn less than men, controlling the human capital factors? How does

Table 4.2   *Standardized least squares estimates for the relations between human capital factors, biographic variables and job level and income (n = 389, stepwise model fitting)*

	Net income t_2	Job level t_2	$t_1 - t_2$ job change	Net income t_1	Job level t_1
Job level t_2	.14**				
$t_1 - t_2$ change		.70***			
Income t_1	.44***				
Job level t_1		.91***		.12**	
Change × income t_1	-.19***	.13**			
Change × job level t_1		-.54***			
Education	.13**	.13***			.37***
Experience					.27***
Age				.61***	.39***
Gender[a]	-.28***			-.11**	.08*
R^2	.34	.64	.00	.46	.32
F	40.65	141.25		110.06	46.54

[a] high = female, * = $p < .05$, ** = $p < .01$, *** = $p < .001$.

the income of men and women develop across time? Do the male–female income differences persist, become lower, or even larger?

These questions were explored using least squares regression analysis. The sample consisted of 389 young adults (49 per cent female, mean age 22.4 years, on average 2.5 years of labor market experience) who were employed full-time. Table 4.2 presents the results. As hypothesized, job level was an important determinant of income at both occasions. Time 2 income was – obviously – strongly affected by time 1 income; this stability effect was weaker when a job change had occurred. From the biographic variables, level of education turned out to be an important asset indeed, in that it determined across-time income growth. Finally, and most interestingly, gender strongly determined time 2 income. Men had a higher income than women; although a similar effect was also found at time 1, the negative effect of gender was much stronger at time 2 (-.28 versus -.11). This analysis, therefore, provides evidence that the male–female income gap was widening across time. How this finding is interpreted depends on the investigator's theoretical vantage point; some may attribute this result to discriminatory tendencies, while others may believe that women tend to attach less importance to pursuing a career.

Technical considerations in the specification of the model and in interpreting the results   As the reader will have noted, the above example employed the regressor variable approach rather than the difference score method. Although in principle the difference score approach could have been used (the time 1 minus time 2 difference reflecting income growth across time, a quantity that fits the research question rather naturally), the model contained a time 1 income × job change interaction effect. This effect could not have been estimated using the difference score strategy; therefore, the regressor variable approach was preferred.

Further, we felt there was little reason to expect ceiling effects, as there is no upper boundary to the income variable. However, regression to the mean might have occurred. In order to examine this possibility, we first computed the average time 1 and time 2 income for the full sample. The average time 1 income was Dfl. 2,150 (SD = 750; Dfl. 1 equals about .50 US$), and the average time 2 income was Dfl. 3,050. Successively the participants who were at least one standard deviation above the average time 1 income were selected (n = 40). The average income for this subsample at time 1 was Dfl. 3,500, and their average time-2-income was Dfl. 4,100. Hence, at time 1 the difference between the overall mean income and the average of the best-earning subsample was (Dfl. 3,500 minus Dfl. 2,150 equals) Dfl. 1,350; at time 2, the difference between the overall group mean and the average income for this group was only Dfl. 1,050. Hence, the participants who earned a relatively high income at time 1 were closer to the group mean at time 2, which means that regression to the mean occurred. In order to control this effect, an investigator might select the participants who did not have an extremely low or high income, re-analyze the data set, and compare the results to those presented in Table 4.2. This would reveal whether and to which degree regression to the mean biased the results.

Assessing causal direction across time: cross-lagged panel analysis

Variables may mutually influence each other. For example, developmental psychologists have long assumed that parents 'socialize' their children – that is, that they transmit their own values to their offspring (e.g., Taris, Semin and Bok, 1998). On the other hand, however, it would seem likely that children can also influence their parents' attitudes and values; children may challenge their parents' beliefs and attitudes, which may lead parents to reconsider (and possibly alter) these. Both effects seem plausible a priori: it is difficult to come up with a unidirectional theoretical model specifying why parents influence the attitudes of their children, and why the reverse effect is implausible. Building on the work of Lazarsfeld (1946/1972), Campbell and Stanley (1963) suggested a solution for this problem by proposing the *cross-lagged panel correlation* methodology (CLPC).

Figure 4.3 shows the basic two-variable, two-wave cross-lagged panel model. Variables A and B were measured twice, at time 1 and time 2. Six different correlations can be computed for these four variables: two synchronous correlations (each variable with the other at the same point in

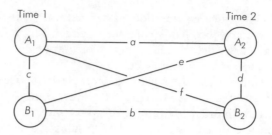

Figure 4.3   *The two-wave, two-variable cross-lagged panel model*

time; lines c and d in Figure 4.3), two autocorrelations (each variable with itself at two points in time, lines a and b), and two cross-lagged correlations (each variable with the other at a different point in time, that is, lines e and f, Kenny and Harackiewicz, 1979). The general idea behind CLPC is that comparison of the cross-lagged correlations is indicative of the causal priority of the variables. For example, if the correlation between A_1 and B_2 is significantly stronger than the correlation between A_2 and B_1, one would conclude that A has causal priority over B. If the cross-lagged correlations are about equal, then the relation between A and B was spurious (Campbell and Stanley, 1963; Kenny, 1975).

In the early days of CLPC, researchers thought that it was sufficient to compare the cross-lagged correlations A_1–B_2 and B_1–A_2. However, it has been shown that such an approach can yield very misleading results. The basic fault of comparing cross-lagged correlations lies in the fact that these do not exclusively reflect the lagged causal effects of one variable on another. The association between two such variables can also be due to the fact that they are both correlated to a third variable; controlling this third variable may reveal that no association between the first two variables remains. For example, in Figure 4.3 the correlation between A_1 and B_2 may disappear after controlling B_1 (and, possibly, A_2). Failing to control for these other effects can severely bias the results.

Cross-lagged panel analysis

A safer approach for assessing the causal priority among a pair of variables was proposed by Kessler and Greenberg (1981), who used regression analysis to estimate the cross-lagged effects. In this approach, two regression equations are fitted. In the first, A_2 is regressed on A_1 and B_1 (thus, this is an instance of the regressor variable approach discussed earlier on; see Figure 4.2(b)). The second regression equation has B_2 as the dependent variable and B_1 and A_1 as predictors (of course, the model may include other predictors as well). The standardized regression estimates of the effect of A_1 on B_2, and of

Table 4.3 *Correlations among mother and child attitudes towards premarital sex at two occasions, as a function of their mutual understanding*

	High mutual understanding (n = 128)			
	t_1 attitude child	t_2 attitude child	t_1 attitude mother	t_2 attitude mother
t_1 attitude child	1.00			
t_2 attitude child	.47	1.00		
t_1 attitude mother	.69	.21	1.00	
t_2 attitude mother	.01	.21	.16	1.00
	Low mutual understanding (n = 127)			
	t_1 attitude child	t_2 attitude child	t_1 attitude mother	t_2 attitude mother
t_1 attitude child	1.00			
t_2 attitude child	.05	1.00		
t_1 attitude mother	.53	.01	1.00	
t_2 attitude mother	.01	.40	.09	1.00

NB: Correlations of .17 and over significant at $p < .05$.

B_1 on A_2 can then be compared; if either of these is significantly larger than the other (taking into account the size of the standard errors), we can conclude about the causal priority of A versus B. The gain of this approach compared to CLPC is that in the first the time 1–time 2 stability effects are controlled; in the second, this across-time stability is neglected.

Consider the correlations presented in Table 4.3 as an example. This table presents the correlations among the attitudes of mother and child toward premarital sex (a six-item scale, with items such as 'It is all right to have sex before marriage if the partners love each other' and 'it is o.k. to have sex with somebody you have met recently and don't know very well, as long as both of you are attracted to each other' (1 = 'disagree strongly', 7 = 'agree strongly'). This scale was included in a two-wave panel study among a sample of 253 British adolescent–mother pairs (mean age adolescent 15.8 years). Further, the adolescents answered several items concerning the degree to which they felt that their mother understood them well (such as 'my mother always listens to what I say'). On the basis of their responses on this scale, the sample was divided into a low and a high mutual understanding group. The principal question to be answered was, How do mother and child affect each other's attitudes toward premarital sex, and to what degree does this vary as a function of their degree of mutual understanding?

Table 4.3 reveals that for the low mutual understanding group there was little reason to assume that mother and child mutually influenced each other (the cross-lagged correlations were both equal to .01 and did not differ significantly from zero). For the high mutual understanding group, however, the correlation between mother's attitude at time 1 and their child's attitude at time 2 was significant (.21, $p < .05$). As the corresponding correlation between the child's attitude at time 1 and the mother's attitude at time 2 was not significant (.01, *ns*, the difference between these two correlations was significant at $p < .05$), it seemed safe to conclude that mothers transmit their attitude towards premarital sex to their children, such that if the mother holds positive attitudes toward premarital sex, it is likely that their child will hold positive attitudes toward this issue as well.

To check whether these casual impressions about the causal priority of the sexual attitudes of mother and child could be retained, two structural equation models were fitted to the data (Jöreskog and Sörbom, 1993), for the low and high mutual understanding group separately. In comparison to ordinary least-squares regression analysis, this procedure has the advantage that the two regression equations (one for the time 2 attitudes of the mother, and the other for the time 2 attitudes of the child) can be estimated simultaneously. The results of these analyses are presented graphically in Figure 4.4. The figure confirms that there were no cross-lagged effects for the low mutual understanding group (the estimates for the lagged effects are not significantly different from zero). Thus, for this group there is no reason to assume that either mother or child influences the other's attitudes toward premarital sex. However, this is different in the high mutual group. The analyses reveal that there is a lagged causal effect from the mother's attitude on her child's attitude towards premarital sex. However, contrary to the impression based on the respective correlation coefficient (of .21), the standardized estimate for this effect is negative ($-.15$, $p < .05$). Thus, controlling their initial score on the attitude toward premarital sex, adolescents with mothers holding positive (negative) attitudes toward premarital sex tended to obtain lower (higher) scores at time 2, relative to other adolescents (but note that the stability of the attitude toward premarital sex was quite impressive). Thus, whereas the views of mother and child coincided rather strongly at time 1 (as evidenced by a .47 correlation, Figure 4.4), their views tended to diverge as the child matures. Children of mothers holding a positive (liberal) attitude towards premarital sex became somewhat less positive in this respect; the reverse applied to adolescents with mothers holding a traditional attitude toward premarital sex. In effect, the variance in adolescent attitudes toward premarital sex decreased across time. In the first part of this chapter this was denoted as regression toward the mean; the interesting thing is, of course, that this regression depended on the time-1 attitudes of the mother.

The least that these analyses show is that a comparison of cross-lagged correlation effects may yield misleading results. Not controlling the stability effects may well give rise to erroneous results (see Rogosa, 1988, for more examples). Of course, one could devise strategies to deal with these problems. For example, the influence of third variables on the association between two variables could be 'partialled out' – that is, the correlation between two variables could be computed, net of their correlation due to the

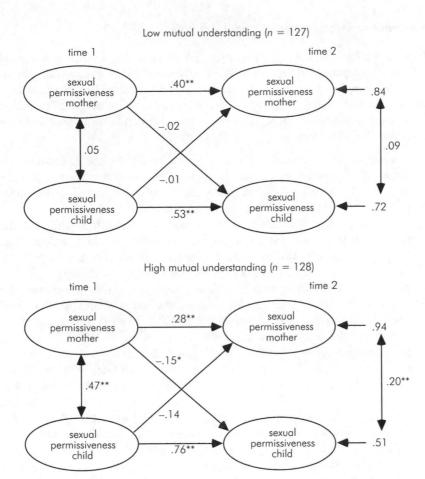

Figure 4.4 *Standardized LISREL-estimates for a cross-lagged panel model for the reciprocal effects between sexual attitudes of mother and child as a function of their mutual understanding.* * = p < .05, ** = p < .01

third variable (Blalock, 1962). However, as conducting a regression analysis is currently just as easy as computing a correlation matrix, such strategies make little sense. The practice of comparing cross-correlations originates from the dark middle ages of empirical social and behavioral science; a time when computers were scarce and slow, and when statistical analyses usually had to be done by hand. In such circumstances, taking a shortcut by comparing cross-correlations might be considered defensible. However, currently there is no lack of computer power, which knocks the bottom out of the 'scarcity' argument; there is no need to turn to an ad-hoc response to a problem that has become obsolete.

Assumptions of cross-lagged panel analysis

Apart from the issue of whether investigators should examine cross-lagged correlations or standardized regression coefficients (this issue is unambiguously resolved by now), there are several other problems and perhaps too-strong assumptions in cross-lagged panel analysis. Shingles (1985) provided an extensive review of these. The most important problems and assumptions are the following.

1 *Continuity*. It is assumed that the causal processes are continuous or ongoing as opposed to unique or abrupt. Therefore, the causal process may be observed (at least in part) during any temporal interval, irrespective of the timing of the waves of a study.

2 *Finite causal lag*. It is assumed that cause precedes effect, and that the causal process does not occur instantaneously but with a finite lag. Clearly, some period of time must elapse before a cause can take effect, or else CLPA cannot be of any help in sorting out causality.

3 *Congruence of measurement and causal lags*. The interval between the observations must approximately be of the same length as the 'true' causal lag – that is, the period that it takes for the cause to take effect. The larger the discrepancy, the lower the chance that CLPA will reveal the underlying causal process. If the interval between the waves of the study is too small, insignificant parameter estimates will be found because the causal process has not yet had enough time to unfold itself. A too-large interval will lead to biased results as well (Raffalovich and Knoke, 1983; Sandefur and Tuma, 1987). For example, changes are often repeatable; participants may change their attitudes several times during a particular period of time. If a variable affects another variable only temporarily, the same score on two consecutive measurements of this variable may be found – even if in the meantime the score on this variable was different. Hence, it is imperative that the time lag between the waves of a study closely approximates the real causal lag. However, as the length of this causal lag is usually unknown, it may be difficult to satisfy this assumption.

4 *Equality of causal lags*. Further, the time that variable A needs to affect B may be longer or shorter than the time that B needs to affect A. If so, it is obviously impossible that the measurement lag equates to the causal lag for *both* causal processes. For example, B may need less time to affect A than A needs to affect B, even if their causal effects are actually equally strong. If a short interval between the waves is chosen, we are likely to conclude that the effect of B on A is stronger than the reverse effect.

One puzzling finding in CLPA is that the results tend to depend on the length of the time lag between the waves of the study. Table 4.4 illustrates

Table 4.4 *Standardized least squares estimates of a cross-lagged panel analysis (n = 647) after one year, two years and four years (three separate analyses, one for each time lag); cross-lagged effects in italics*

	First analysis: one year later		Second analysis: two years later		Third analysis: four years later	
	Employed time 2	Child present time 2	Employed time 2	Child present time 2	Employed time 2	Child present time 2
Has partner time 1	.07***	.08***	.04**	.15***	-.00	.20***
Level of education	.31***	.00	.21**	.02	.17*	.10
Socio-economic status	-.05	-.01	-.04	-.01	-.05	-.06
Emancipation attitude	.01	-.02	-.03	.01	.00	.01
Employed time 1	.36***	*-.03*	.32***	*.02*	.13**	*.02*
Child present time 1	*-.13***	.85***	*-.17***	.75***	*-.22***	.63***
R^2	.45	.78	.31	.62	.16	.49

* $p < .05$, ** $p < .01$, *** $p < .001$.

this issue. Here the regression approach to CLPA was used to estimate the reciprocal and lagged effects between women's employment status (employed vs not employed) and the presence of children. The causal priority between these variables is uncertain. Experience shows that it is quite likely that employed women will leave the labor market if they become mothers. Alternatively, women might postpone pregnancy in favor of pursuing a career (Waite and Stolzenberg, 1976). To resolve this issue, at four points in time measurements were taken of the employment status of 647 employed Dutch women aged 18 to 30 years. Further, it was examined whether they had any children. The first wave of the study was conducted in 1987; the next three waves were conducted one year, two years, and four years later, respectively. This study included several control variables as well, but these are of little interest here.

Focusing on a one-year interval between the first and the second wave, it turns out that the presence of children has a negative effect on employment status. The other cross-lagged effect (from employment status at time 1 on the presence of children at time 2) does not significantly differ from zero. Thus, it appears that the presence of children leads to a withdrawal from the labor market, while there is no reason to assume that employment delays having children.

Although these conclusions do not alter when the two- and four-year intervals are considered, it is clear that in time the presence of children at time 1 becomes an increasingly important predictor of a change in employment status: from −.13 for a one-year interval, via −.17 for a two-year lag, to −.22 for a four-year interval (note that the effects of the other variables vary substantially across time as well). This is a fairly common finding in CLPA (Raffalovich and Knoke, 1983; Rogosa, 1988; Sandefur and Tuma, 1987). The latter two studies reveal that not only do the effect sizes vary considerably across time lags, but that the direction of these effects may also be subject to change. Clearly, analyzing the 'right' measurement lag is imperative in CLPA. However, as the true causal lag is rarely known, it is difficult to know whether this assumption has been satisfied. In this context, Sandefur and Tuma (1987) suggest that the results of a cross-lagged panel analysis should always be reported in relation to the measurement interval in this particular study, as the findings of a CLPA cannot be generalized beyond the specific measurement interval used in the study. For example, the conclusion of the above study might be that 'the presence of children is a better predictor of employment status than employment status of the presence of children, at least for a two-year measurement interval'.

Further reading

The issues discussed in this chapter have been the subject of quite a body of research. Many statisticians have considered the use of change scores. From a historical point of view, Cronbach and Furby's (1970) article is perhaps of most interest. The ideas expressed in this paper, however, have been shown to be largely incorrect (Rogosa, 1988; Allison, 1990). Rogosa's (1988) paper on several 'myths' about longitudinal research summarizes the main findings of his important work on this issue in a reasonably accessible manner. Kessler and Greenberg's (1981) textbook is still an important source of suitable statistical models for the analysis of discrete-time panel data, as is Hsiao's (1986) book.

The models discussed in this chapter are well-suited for the analysis of panel studies involving a limited number of waves. That is, the models discussed here soon become very complicated when applied to panel studies involving, say, more than three or four waves. Some time ago, McArdle and Aber (1990) proposed to analyze such multi-wave panel data by means of growth curve analysis. The general idea is that across-time growth curves can be characterized in terms of two parameters only, namely a constant and a slope parameter, the latter representing the rate of increase or the decrease of the scores across time. Although this approach requires a fair amount of familiarity with structural equation models, it is a potentially interesting approach to modeling across-time growth for multi-wave panel data. Interested readers may consult Patterson (1993) and Rovine and Von Eye (1991); the first author presents a reasonably compact introduction to this issue, while the latter two authors present a full-size application, including details on the LISREL output. Neither text, however, is easy to comprehend.

5   Analysis of Repeated Measures

This chapter discusses the application of multivariate analysis of variance in the context of non-experimental longitudinal survey research. Many introductory textbooks on statistical analysis provide excellent introductions to the analysis of data obtained by means of a 'repeated measures' design (a design in which measures are repeatedly taken during a particular time interval from the same set of participants – thus, a panel study, following the definition presented in Chapter 1). It is usually assumed that the data are collected in carefully controlled and balanced laboratory experiments. However, investigators may also use analysis of variance when they analyze data collected via a non-experimental longitudinal survey design, although some drawbacks must be taken for granted. These are addressed in this chapter.

Examining across-time growth

One of the great virtues of repeated measures data is that they can conveniently be displayed in easy-to-interpret plots. For example, Figure 5.1 shows measurements of calves' weights taken on 11 occasions after the start of an experiment on the control of intestinal parasites. The vertical axis shows their weight (in pounds) and the horizontal axis shows days elapsed since the start of the experiment. The values for individual calves are connected by straight lines. In general, the weight of the calves increases with time (as the overall positive slope of the plots shows). Further, the calves follow different paths (even after allowing some irregularity). Whereas the difference between the body weights of the calves at the start of the experiment was relatively small (ranging from roughly 225 to 275 pounds), this difference increased across time (after 133 days, the lowest body weight was about 260 pounds, the highest about 360 pounds). Such a 'fan shape', showing increasing variance across time, is typical of growth curves. Finally, note that two calves are outliers, starting at a low weight, remaining low, and ending with a sharp decline in body weight.

Visual inspection of plots such as those presented in Figure 5.1 does not require any special training. However, as Hand and Crowder (1996) put it, we want to go beyond making general statements about the apparent behavior of the units being studied. We want to quantify their behavior, we

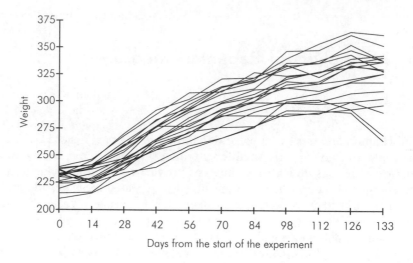

Figure 5.1   *Weights of calves in an experiment on the control of intestinal parasites on 11 occasions after the start of this experiment. (Data adapted from Kenward, 1987; Hand and Crowder, 1996, Table B.23)*

want to describe it accurately, and we want to compare the behavior of different groups of units. Repeated-measures analysis of variance (ANOVA) is a statistical technique that allows us to accomplish this.

Analysis of variance: some basics

The statistical analysis of the data obtained in a typical experimental study is relatively simple. The researcher assigns the participants in the study to the experimental and control conditions either randomly or on the basis of a subject-matching procedure, thus ensuring that the experimental and control groups do not differ substantially, apart from the treatment (or 'manipulation') they are about to receive. For example, groups of cancer patients may receive different dosages of a particular drug, chicks may follow different protein diets, etc. Further, the investigator controls the number of participants that are assigned to each 'cell' in the design; the idea is that each (combination of) treatment(s) is received by equal numbers of participants (if so, the design is *completely balanced*).

The data obtained by means of experimental designs are usually analyzed using analysis of variance, and the effects of the manipulations are often expressed in terms of the differences between the means obtained for each of the conditions. For example, employment advertisements often contain a section that describes the personal characteristics of the desired applicant, not only in terms of the desired level of education and amount of experience, but also in terms of traits such as 'analytical skills' and 'creativity'. One common finding is that such person characteristics are usually considered to be more typical for males than for females (e.g., managerial capacities), or more typical for females than for males (for example, communicative skills). Taris and Bok (1998) were interested in the effects of inclusion of such gender-specific person characteristics in employment advertisements on the attributions of male and female judges. Would the gender-specificity of such person characteristics influence their judgements of the attractiveness of the job being advertised?

Taris and Bok designed three hypothetical employment advertisements, which differed only in the type of personal characteristics that the desired applicant should possess. The 'male' advertisement stated that applicants should possess 'resolution', 'entrepreneurial skills', 'managerial capacities', 'commercial feeling', and 'analytical skills'. The 'female' employment advertisement, in turn, mentioned 'creativity', 'communicative skills', 'ability to make others enthusiastic', 'customer oriented', and 'ability to motivate others'. Finally, there was a 'neutral' advertisement that did not mention any person characteristics at all. Extensive pre-testing revealed that these person characteristics indeed differed in terms of their applicability to 'typical' males and females.

This stimulus material was included in a simple two-factor experiment. One factor was Gender of participant (male vs female); the other was Advertisement type (with three levels: neutral advertisement vs 'male' advertisement vs 'female' advertisement). Note that only Advertisement type was a true experimental factor, as participant gender could obviously not be manipulated by the investigator.

One important decision that then had to be taken was whether each participant would judge all employment advertisements (Condition would then be a *within-participants* factor), or that each participant would judge only one of the three advertisements (Advertisement type would then be a *between-participants* factor).

Between-participants analysis of variance

Assume that the effects of the gender-specificity of employment advertisements are analyzed as a between-participants factor. Thus, each participant in the study would rate one and only one advertisement; care must be taken that the study is completely balanced (thus, that each advertisement is judged by equal numbers of male and female participants). The score of participant k on the dependent variable (attractiveness of the vacancy, as rated on a 100-point scale) can be decomposed as follows:

$$y_{ijk} = \mu + \alpha_i + \beta_j + \alpha\beta_{ij} + \varepsilon_{ijk}, \tag{5.1}$$

with y_{ijk} denoting the score of participant k, μ denoting the average attractiveness regardless of condition, α_i denoting the effect of condition a_i (Advertisement type; neutral vs female vs male advertisement), β_j denoting the effect of condition b_j (Gender: male vs female), $\alpha\beta_{ij}$ denoting the effect of the Advertisement type by Gender interaction effect, and ε_{ijk} representing the possible effects of other factors than Type of advertisement or Gender (for example, some participants may rate a vacancy as unattractive, perhaps because they feel that their own type or level of education does not match the type of education mentioned in the advertisement).

For all of the effects in (5.1) – with the exception of ε_{ijk} – we can compute whether this effect is significantly different from zero. Generally, the testing procedure amounts to partitioning the total variance (the sum of the squared differences from the mean (SS_{total}) into distinct sums of squares that pertain to the effect of Advertisement type ($SS_{Advertisement\ type}$), Gender (SS_{Gender}), the Advertisement type by Gender interaction ($SS_{Advertisement\ type\ \times\ Gender}$), and error variance ($SS_{error}$). As virtually every introductory statistics textbook describes in detail how to compute the appropriate effect sizes, degrees of freedom, and associated F-values, the formulas to compute these are not presented here. Rather, we refer to classic textbooks such as Winkler and Hays (1971) and Winer (1971), and more recent updates of these.

Within-participants analysis of variance

One distinguishing feature of between-participants designs as opposed to within-participants designs is that in the first type of design many participants are needed to warrant that the statistical tests have sufficient statistical power. A rule of thumb is that each cell of the design should contain at least ten participants. Thus, in the 2 (Gender: male vs female) × 3 (Advertisement type: neutral vs male vs female) design at least sixty participants are needed to obtain sufficient statistical power (Ito, 1980). Although this figure is not excessively high, the number of participants needed can be reduced if a within-participants design is used for Advertisement type. Instead of judging only one employment advertisement, each participant then judges all three advertisements. Applying the 'ten participants per cell' rule, only twenty participants would be needed for the study.

Example. In the Taris and Bok study, 52 student judges (24 males and 28 females) rated the attractiveness of all three employment advertisements. Figure 5.2 presents the average attractiveness ratings of the three advertisements, each separately for male and female judges.

This analysis constitutes an example of repeated measures analysis of variance, as each participant rated the attractiveness of all employment advertisements. An ANOVA with the three attractiveness ratings as the

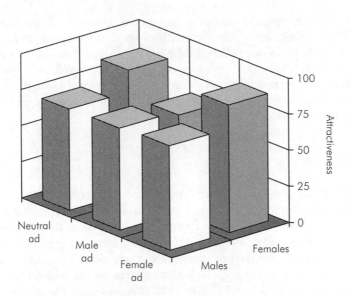

Figure 5.2   *Perceived attractiveness of a vacancy as a function of Gender and Condition (after Taris and Bok, 1998, Study 3)*

dependent variables (thus, with Advertisement type being a within-participants factor) and Gender as a between-participants variable revealed main effects for Gender (the women found the positions on average more attractive than the men did) and Advertisement type (the male position was judged to be less attractive than the other two positions). Finally, the Gender by Advertisement type interaction was also significant, with the men finding all vacancies about equally attractive, whereas the women were attracted most to the female and neutral vacancies.

Analysis of longitudinal designs

In the comparison between between- and within-participants analysis of variance above, we especially focused on the advantages of the latter with respect to the efficiency of gathering and analyzing data. Although the example given above complies with the standard definition of longitudinal data (in the sense of repeatedly measuring a particular concept for the same set of participants, Chapter 1), it is atypical for a longitudinal data set in that there is no natural order in the sequence in which the participants judged the attractiveness of the advertisements (indeed, the order of presentation was randomized across participants). Few investigators will consider these data as longitudinal.

However, the repeated measures mode of analysis of variance described above is also well suited for the analysis of data sets that comply more closely with the definition of longitudinal data provided above. For example, Figure 5.1 presented data on calves' weights as measured on 11 occasions. This data set corresponds more closely with the concept of longitudinal data. Yet, with some extensions this data set can also be analyzed quite well with analysis of variance.

Contrast analysis

The factors in any analysis of variance consist of different levels or categories. For example, hair color (with categories brown, blonde, black, red, grey and white) is one such factor; being in one of three experimental groups may be another. In principle, we may have no expectations what-soever regarding the differences between the levels of a particular factor; for which category we might find the highest scores on the dependent variable, for which categories we will obtain similar scores, and for which category the lowest score will be found. Alternatively, we may have strong a priori hypotheses regarding the pattern of differences among the groups. As regards within-participant factors, there may be a 'natural order' in the levels of this factor. Again, consider the growth curves presented in Figure 5.1. It would seem natural to compare the levels of the consecutive meas-urements of the calves' weights to obtain insight in the pattern of growth across time. Such questions can be dealt with using contrast analysis.

What is a contrast?   A contrast on a set of g groups is any set of g numbers which sum to zero. This sounds admittedly rather abstract, but the general idea can easily be understood by way of some examples. Consider a four-group study on the effects of various dosages of a particular drug. Three groups receive three different dosages of this drug: the fourth group serves as a control group. The first question might be whether there are differ-ences between the effects of the three dosages; if not, our second question could be whether there are any differences between the three experimental groups and the control group. To test the first question, the means of the low dosage group might be compared with those of the medium dosage group, and those of the medium dosage group to the means obtained for the high dosage group. The corresponding contrasts are shown as i and ii in Table 5.1. As the reader may check, each of these contrasts sum to zero. The first contrast describes the difference between the low and the medium dosage group (thus, the high dosage group and the control group are not of interest), while the second describes the difference between the medium and high dosage groups (the low dosage and control group not of interest). If these comparisons fail to reveal differences between the groups, a third

Table 5.1 *Contrasts among four groups in a study of the effects of drug dosage*

	Dosage			
Contrast	Low	Medium	High	Nothing
i	1	-1	0	0
ii	0	1	-1	0
iii	1	1	1	-3

i: low vs medium dosage
ii: medium vs high dosage
iii: any dosage vs no dosage

contrast might be tested, namely that numbered iii in Table 5.1, which describes the difference between the first three (experimental) groups, and the control group. Again, this contrast sums to zero.

Contrasts can be put on between- as well as within-participant factors, and they are extremely handy in testing hypotheses. They are also very handy for analyzing longitudinal studies, especially when we have more than two measurements of a particular variable across time. For example, assume that a particular variable has been measured at three equally spaced waves of a study (Figure 5.3). One potentially interesting analysis would focus on the contrast (1, 0, −1), which compares the mean of the participants' scores at wave 1 (point A in Figure 5.3) to their average scores at wave 3 (point B). If this contrast is significant, the participants' scores have changed across time.

Although comparison of wave 1 and wave 3 tells us whether there is across-time change, it does not inform us about the *rate* at which the response has changed (indeed, two-wave studies cannot be informative about the shape of the growth curves by definition, which led Rogosa, 1988, to conclude that a two-wave longitudinal study is better than a cross-sectional study, but not very much so). It might be that the participants' scores have increased linearly across time. If so, one would expect the mean score at time 2 to equal the average of the participants' scores at time 1 and time 3 (point C in Figure 5.3). This calls for a contrast that compares the average mean scores at time 1 and time 3 to the mean score at time 2, for example (−1, 2, −1). Assume that the mean score at time 2 equals point D in Figure 5.3. D is clearly not on the straight line that connects A with B. The question, of course, is whether D differs significantly from C (which represents the expected mean score at time 2 if there is only linear change across time).

It is probably clear that as the number of waves of a study increases, more complex patterns of across-time change can be tested. That is, whereas a simple two-wave panel study merely allows us to see whether some form of change has occurred across time, a three-wave study enables

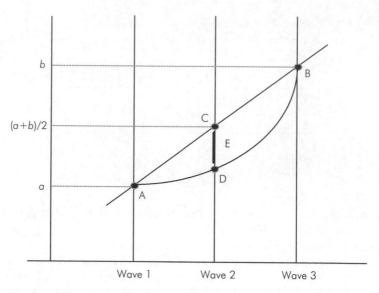

Figure 5.3   *Linear and quadratic trends in a three-wave longitudinal study*

the investigator to check whether this change occurred linearly across time (that is, a test of whether the pattern of change was quadratic). A four-wave study would allow for testing linear, quadratic and cubic patterns of change; a five-wave study would, in addendum, allow for a test of a quartic pattern of change; and so forth. Clearly, specifying the correct contrasts for analyzing the pattern of across-time change can become very complex for multiple-wave studies (see Hand and Taylor, 1987, and Hand and Crowder, 1996, for thorough discussions of contrast analysis). Fortunately, current statistical programs contain many preset contrasts, which certainly makes an investigator's life easier.

Example: analysis of growth curves   Take, as an example, the growth curves presented in Figure 5.1. Actually, the data for this example were collected for two groups of calves. Figure 5.4 shows the growth curves for these two groups separately. There are several interesting differences between these two groups. It seems that the variance in the first group increases across time, whereas the growth curves in the second group all more or less parallel each other. Further, the weights of the calves differ across groups. At the first wave, the average weight of the calves in the first group is about 260 pounds; the corresponding figure in the second group is substantially lower, namely about 230 pounds. The same applies for the other occasions; the calves in the first group seem on average substantially heavier than the calves in the second group. In other respects, however, the shape of the growth curves is about the same.

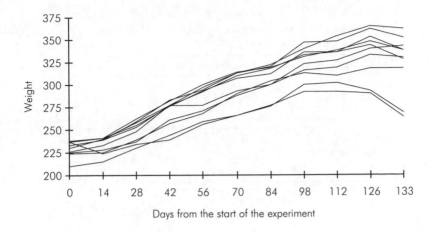

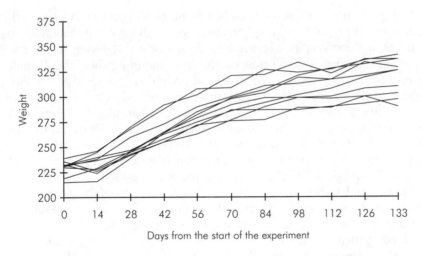

Figure 5.4   *Weights of calves in an experiment on the control of intestinal parasites on 11 occasions after the start of this experiment, for two different groups (data adapted from Kenward, 1987)*

In principle, we would like to answer three basic questions (Hand and Crowder, 1996). First, are the weights of the two groups of calves (averaged across occasions) at the same level; thus, is there a 'group effect'? Second, are the 11 consecutive measurements of the calves' weights the same (is there a 'time effect')? Third, is the pattern of the growth curves the same for each group (is there a 'group by time interaction')? Given that there are 11 measurements available, very complex growth curves could have been examined. For simplicity, however, we limited our attention to the linear, quadratic, and cubic effects.

Table 5.2   *Parameter estimates for the contrasts testing the linear, quadratic, and cubic components of across-time weight change*

Estimates for the linear effect	Estimate	Standard error	T-value
Time	110.72	5.00	22.10
Group by Time	8.90	5.00	1.77
Estimates for the quadratic effect			
Time	-22.51	2.36	-9.50
Group by Time	.64	2.36	.27
Estimates for the cubic effect			
Time	-11.03	1.83	-6.02
Group by Time	-6.03	1.83	-3.29

As regards the first question, there was no main effect of Group: multivariate $F(1,18) < 1.00$, *ns*. Thus, the two groups did not differ significantly in terms of their weights, averaged across occasions. Relevant to the third question, there was a significant Group by Time interaction effect: multivariate $F(10,9) = 3.68$, $p < .05$. Thus, although the groups did not differ significantly in terms of their weights averaged across occasions, the shape of the growth curves differed across groups. Regarding the Time effect (question 2), there was a very significant main effect of Time: multivariate $F(10,9) = 71.16$, $p < .001$, evidencing that there were substantial differences between the weights of the calves at different occasions. Thus, we could proceed by inspection of the univariate parameter estimates for the linear, quadratic, and cubic components of change with time. As there was a significant interaction with Group, these effects were also considered.

Table 5.2 shows the parameter estimates for the linear, quadratic and cubic components of across-time change in weight. The linear, quadratic, and cubic components were all significant, which is reasonable given the growth curves presented in Figure 5.4. The significant Group by Time interaction effect was obtained from the cubic component; the other two interactions were not significant.

Analysis of variance for longitudinal survey data

As the reader may have concluded from the preceding sections, analysis of variance is quite attractive for analyzing longitudinal data gathered within an experimental framework. The technique is relatively simple, flexible, and it can be used to answer many different types of research questions. Moreover, any statistical computer program offers all of the possibilities discussed above – and many more as a bonus. However, some problems arise when it comes to the analysis of non-experimental survey data by means of ANOVA. These are (a) the degree to which the 'experimental manipulations' are controlled by the investigator; (b) problems of sample size, power, and error; and (c) the assumption of equal numbers of observations in each cell of the design.

The manipulations are not under control of the investigator   In a well-conducted laboratory experiment, anything that happens is controlled by the investigator. All manipulations have carefully been designed by the experimenter, and nothing unforeseen should occur. This is quite different in a non-experimental context. Here the 'manipulations' of interest occur more or less naturally. For example, we may want to examine the consequences of losing one's spouse for the physical and psychological well-being of people (Stroebe and Stroebe, 1993). A sample of couples is followed in a longitudinal study. At all waves of the study measures are taken of their physical and psychological well-being. Given enough time, a substantial proportion of the participants will be confronted with the death of their spouse during the study. Thus, the design is a version of Campbell and Stanley's (1963) non-equivalent control group design. The study consists of two (or more) waves, two criterion measures (psychological and physical well-being), and two groups: an 'experimental' group (the manipulation being the death of one's spouse), and a control group (those participants who did not lose their partner during the interval between the waves of the study).

The point here is that the manipulation of interest was not (and, indeed, *could not* have been) induced by the investigator. As a consequence, the precise nature of the manipulation is not known. Some persons in the experimental group may have lost their partner due to an unforeseen accident, while for others the end may not have come unexpectedly, as their partner suffered from a chronic and deadly disease. It may well be the case that there are distinct differences between the reactions of participants whose partner died unexpectedly, and those who were prepared for this loss. If this factor (expectedness of the loss of the partner) is not controlled, it may very well be that the effects of two qualitatively different manipulations (expected vs unexpected death of the spouse) are confounded. Thus, the *nature* of the manipulation must be considered carefully in advance.

Further, the *timing* of the manipulation is also beyond the investigator's control. Some of the participants who lose their partners will have experienced this loss almost immediately after the first wave of the study has been completed, whereas others will experience this event shortly before the follow-up wave is conducted. The first group may have had ample time to control their grief, whereas the latter may still be in the process of coping with this event. This may lead to large and uncontrolled within-group differences.

Taken together, both issues may cause the error on the manipulation to be quite substantial, up to the point that the results cannot be considered informative as to the hypothesis being tested – do we *really* know why the participants whose spouse died feel so miserable? Have we tested the process of interest, or are other – uncontrolled – factors responsible for the results? The take-home message is that investigators should consider the 'manipulation' of interest as well as possible confounding factors in advance (that is, in the design phase of the study), and they should take appropriate measures. For example, in a study on bereavement it is probably a good idea to have a relatively short interval between the waves of the study. Note that this problem (uncontrollability of the nature and timing of the event of interest) is due to the design of the study, and not to the strategy chosen to analyze the data. Thus, similar problems arise when the same data are analyzed using regression analysis or other statistical techniques.

Sample size, power, and error   One reason why analysis of variance is such a powerful analytic strategy in experimental contexts is that all manipulations are under the full control of the investigator, whereas random assignment of participants to the experimental and control groups ensures that there are no systematic differences between these. This implies that usually few – if any – other variables need to be controlled. As a consequence, even relatively few observations are sufficient to obtain enough statistical power for testing the hypotheses of interest.

This is rather different in survey research. Participants are not randomly allocated to experimental and control groups, and manipulations are not under the control of the experimenter. As the groups may differ in many other respects than the manipulation they receive, it often happens that many other variables must be controlled. Additionally, as argued above, the manipulations are usually considerably weaker than the manipulations in experimental research. Thus, the effects in survey research can usually be expected to be quite weak, at least in comparison to those typically obtained in experimental studies. In order to obtain enough statistical power, survey research needs quite large sample size. Die-hard experimenters may consider a 200-participant survey a large-scale study, but this is a rock-bottom estimate: samples of 500 to 1,000 participants are common in survey research.

Of course, this does not only apply to studies in which analysis of variance is used to analyze the data. However, it is appropriate to mention numbers here, as it is likely that those who might think about application of ANOVA to longitudinal survey data are familiar with experiments, and less so with survey research.

Equal numbers of participants in each cell   Analysis of variance assumes that each cell of the design contains about the same numbers of observations. Imagine a two-factor design with factors *A* and *B*, with two categories

Table 5.3   Orthogonal and non-orthogonal designs

(a) Orthogonal design (no dependence between the manipulations)			(b) Non-orthogonal design (dependence between the manipulations)		
	b_1	b_2		b_1	b_2
a_1	25	25	50	10	30	40
a_2	25	25	50	45	15	60
	50	50	100	55	45	100

chi-square with 1 df = .00; p = 1.00   chi-square with 1 df = 24.2; p < .01

each, a_1 and a_2, and b_1 and b_2, respectively. In principle the design should be completely balanced – that is, there should be equal numbers of participants in each cell of the design. If this assumption is satisfied, A and B are independent from each other (they are 'orthogonal'; see Table 5.3(a)).

In survey research the observations are seldom as nicely distributed across the cells as in Table 5.3(a). On the contrary, because the manipulations occur more or less beyond control of the researcher it frequently happens that the cell frequencies differ as strongly as in Table 5.3(b). In this example, there is a strong dependence between A and B, as evidenced by a very significant chi-square value.

This dependence presents problems in the estimation of the effects of factors A and B, in that the results for A and B are dependent upon the order in which they are entered into the equation. Assume that A and B together explain 70 per cent of the variance in the dependent variable(s). It may be the case that if only A is entered, about 50 per cent of the variance is accounted for, leaving only 20 per cent to be explained by B and the $A \times B$ interaction. Thus, B would seem to be of minor importance here. However, if the order of entry is reversed, B may actually turn out to explain 40 per cent, with A and the $A \times B$ interaction accounting for 30 per cent – thus, here A would seem to matter least. Thus, the fact that the design is non-orthogonal results in problems in estimating the effects of A and B.

One solution to this problem is to enter the main effects and interaction terms in a particular theory-based sequence. Unfortunately, it frequently occurs that no particular order may seem especially appropriate; theory may fail us here. Alternatively, investigators may adopt the rule of thumb that main effects should be tested prior to interaction effects, and lower-order interaction effects prior to higher-order interactions (Finn, 1974). However, if the investigator aims to estimate two (or more) main effects or same-order interaction effects, this procedure is not very helpful either. In these cases researchers may estimate each effect only after *all other* effects have been entered in the analysis (the 'regression' approach). For example, the main effect of B would be estimated only after A and the $A \times B$ interaction have been entered in the analysis; the main effect of A would be estimated after B and the $A \times B$ interaction have been entered; whereas the $A \times B$ interaction would be estimated after the main affects of A and B have been entered in the analysis. Obviously, this procedure yields conservative results; but it is far more acceptable to be conservative than to be overly optimistic about the significance of one's findings.

Example: mental well-being of young workers across time

We conclude this chapter with an example concerning the relations between mental well-being and turnover among a sample of 1,301 young workers. The data were collected in a three-wave, six-nation study on the work socialization of young workers (WOSY International Research Group, 1989). All participants were interviewed for the first time within six months after they took on their first job, and they were subsequently interviewed twice, with a year in between these two follow-up waves. At each of the three waves of the study information was collected about attitudes and behavior of the sample, as well as on issues such as job satisfaction and mental health (Goldberg's General Health Questionnaire, 1972). Further, the participants in the study were asked whether they had taken on a new job during the one-year intervals between the three waves.

The principal assumption in this study was that the participants were expected to leave their job if they felt that the new job would improve upon their current job, which, in turn, would lead to a better mental health (see Taris, Bok and Caljé, 1998, for a more elaborate discussion of this reasoning). Based on the information they provided, the participants were assigned to either of four groups;

1   a group consisting of workers who did not take on a different job during the study (the 'stayers', $n = 688$);
2   a group of workers who took on another job between the first and second wave of the study, but remained in this job afterwards ($n = 281$);
3   a group of workers who took on another job between the second and third wave of the study ($n = 144$); and
4   a highly mobile group of workers who at both follow-up waves said that they had taken on another job during the one-year interval preceding the second and third wave ($n = 188$).

The stayers were expected to report the lowest number of health complaints, whereas the other three groups were expected to report more complaints at the wave just preceding a job change. Figure 5.5 shows the means for each of the four groups at each wave of the study.

Figure 5.5 suggests that the number of health complaints increased across time, but that this change did not occur in an entirely linear fashion.

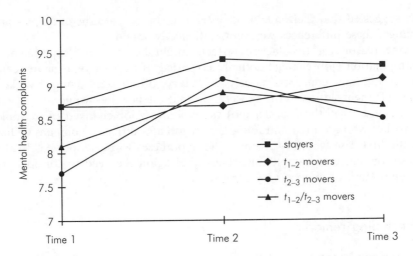

Figure 5.5   *Number of mental health complaints as a function of Time and Job change*

Furthermore, the pattern of change seems to vary across groups. All in all, Figure 5.5 suggests that there may be some – but probably only weak – support for our expectations. To test these impressions, the data were analyzed in a Time (time 1 vs time 2 vs time 3) by Group (stayers vs time 1–2 movers vs time 2–3 movers vs time 1–2 and time 2–3 movers) design, with repeated measures on Time (thus, Time is a within-participants factor) and Group being a between-participant factor. As the study involved three waves, both linear and quadratic effects could be tested.

The analysis yielded significant main effects for Group, multivariate F with (3,1296) df was 2.69, $p < .05$, and Time, multivariate F with (2,1296) df was 9.10, $p < .001$. Further analysis of the main effect for Group revealed that the stayers reported the highest number of health complaints ($M = 9.1$), whereas the means of the other three groups were considerably lower (ranging from 8.4 to 8.8). The main effect for Time was because the participants reported fewer complaints at the first wave of this study ($M = 8.5$) than at the two follow-up waves (average number of health complaints was 9.1 at both occasions).

As the main effect for Time was significant, we may look at the univariate F-tests for the linear and quadratic components of change. The linear component was significant, $F(1,1297) = 11.97$, $p < .001$, underlining that the participants reported more health complaints across time. The quadratic effect was also significant, $F(1,1297) = 7.35$, $p < .01$, suggesting that this across-time change was not completely linear. A look at the plot in Figure 5.5 shows that this is reasonable. Note that the Group by Time interaction was not significant: $F(6,2594) < 1.00$, *ns*. Thus, although Figure

5.5 suggested that there might be differences in the patterns of across-time change, these differences were not statistically sound.

One reason for this lack of effects might be that the 'experimental' manipulation (job change) actually consisted of at least two theoretically rather different concepts, namely voluntary job change (that is, workers who left their old job in the expectation that the new job would improve in some sense upon their former job) vs involuntary job change (for example, a worker who got fired and found a new job at a different company). Only in the first case would one expect the hypotheses to be supported. In this sense, the current example underlines once again the need to consider the manipulation of interest very carefully.

Concluding remarks

The current chapter provided a brief overview of analysis of variance as it may be applied in the context of non-experimental survey research. Despite some problems – pertaining chiefly to the problems presented by 'naturally occurring' experimental manipulations, comparability of the experimental and non-experimental groups, and unequal cell frequencies – it appears that longitudinal survey data may well be analyzed by means of ANOVA. One word of caution, however, is appropriate. If many variables need to be controlled in order to warrant comparability of the groups in one's study, it may well be that MANOVA becomes extremely complicated to perform. In such cases one may better turn to other analytic techniques, such as regression analysis (see Chapter 4).

Further reading

Many introductions to multivariate analysis contain section(s) on (multivariate) analysis of variance. Apart from these general introductions, there is a host of more specialized textbooks. Some of the introductions you might want to consider are Bray and Maxwell (1985) and Iversen and Norpoth (1982). These texts are suitable for relative novices to the field, and present easy-to-follow introductions to the analysis of variance. Winer (1971) is still the standard 600-page reference textbook for analysis of variance. This book contains many practical examples, illustrating the ins and outs of the analysis of (semi-)experimental designs by means of analysis of variance. Ito (1980) presents a useful review of the many test statistics available in (M)ANOVA, as well as their strengths and limitations. David Hand and his co-workers have written several volumes on the analysis of repeated-measures data using analysis of variance. Hand and Taylor (1987) present a non-mathematical and easy to follow introduction to contrast analysis. They include many practical examples, including the commands to be used in several statistical software packages. Crowder and Hand (1990) and Hand and Crowder (1996) are somewhat more sophisticated textbooks, including models that can only be estimated using specialized (and rather exotic) software.

6 Analyzing Durations

This chapter addresses the analysis of duration data. Rather than having measured a qualitative variable at several discrete time points, investigators may have information on the timing of changes in the participants' scores on this variable. If so, the length of the period is known during which the participants in the study belonged to a particular state (that is, how many months they were unemployed, or the length of the time interval between marriage and the birth of a first child). This type of data can be analyzed by means of a class of statistical techniques which are alternately referred to as survival-, failure time-, or event history-analysis. The current chapter deals with these techniques in some detail.

Survival-, failure time-, and event history-analysis

In the preceding chapters we assumed that the scores of the participants in a study were known for a limited number of time points only; their scores between the waves were assumed to be unknown. This was referred to as discrete-time panel analysis, and techniques suitable for analyzing such data were discussed in Chapter 4. However, many processes that may interest the investigator unfold themselves in *continuous* time. That is, changes from one state to another may not only occur at the waves of the study, but also at any moment in between these waves. It is therefore often desirable to measure such processes in a time unit that matches the rate at which the process of interest develops. For example, whereas a transition from unemployment to employment can easily be detected by comparing a person's scores at two adjacent waves of a study (the discrete-time case), the precise moment that this transition occurred can often be pinned down with much more precision. At which month (or even day) did one become employed? The participants in the study are often able and willing to share this information with the investigator – why not take advantage of their knowledge?

Continuous-time data can be collected on many different transitional processes. Consider the following four examples.

- Rao et al. (1998) examined the effects of conventional treatment of head and neck cancers. They found that the overall 5-year survival rate was 20 to 43 per cent for oral cancer, 8 to 25 per cent for pharyngeal

interesting *suicide*
females think about it more,
but males do it more

94   A PRIMER IN LONGITUDINAL DATA ANALYSIS

cancers, and 25 to 62 per cent for laryngeal cancer. This study focused on the survival time of the patient, that is, the time elapsed between the diagnosis of cancer and the death of the patient.

- In a study by Nordström et al. (1995), suicide risk after attempted suicide was examined as a function of sex in a cohort of 1,500 suicide attempters. The suicide mortality after a five-year mean observation period was 6 per cent, with males having twice as high a risk of being successful at a suicide attempt than females.
- Diekmann et al. (1996) conducted a field experiment to explore the relation between the prestige of cars and their drivers' aggression. The investigators had an experimental car block drivers who were waiting at a traffic light. They then recorded the amount of time that elapsed until the drivers responded aggressively by honking their horns or flashing their head lights. They found that drivers in high-prestige cars turned aggressive sooner than those in low-prestige cars.
- Finally, McBride et al. (1998) focused on the duration of homeless spells among persons with severe mental illness. The participants in their study had joined either of two treatment programs for homeless individuals. Those who received assertive community treatment exited the state of being homeless sooner than those who received brokered case management, outpatient treatment, or services from a drop-in center.

Although the techniques discussed in the preceding chapters can to some degree deal with the substantive research questions in these studies, there is a class of statistical techniques that are especially appropriate to analyze this type of data. These techniques are referred to as survival-, failure time-, or event history-analysis. The term *survival analysis* is commonly used in the biomedical sciences. There are often only two states of interest in this discipline: that is, the subjects (guinea pigs, rats, monkeys, human beings, etc.) either die after a certain amount of time, or they are still alive. The subjects in the study have often been diagnosed as suffering from a particular disease, such as cancer or AIDS (in experimental settings such diseases are often induced by the researcher). Belonging to the states of interest (that is, being dead or alive) may be linked to a variety of explanatory variables, such as gender, age, and – of course – treatment variables.

The term *failure time-analysis* is used in reliability analysis of consumer and/or production goods, such as cars, light bulbs, machinery, and the like. The typical research question here is when, and due to which factors, the light bulbs (cars, etc.) 'fail' (break down). The techniques used here are the same as those used in survival analysis, but (as it would seem inappropriate to use terms such as life and death when referring to cars and heating appliances) they are known under a different name.

Finally, in the social and behavioral sciences these techniques are often referred to as *event history-analysis*. Again, a different name applies to the

survived biomedical
failure time consumer/ production
event history social + behavioral
ANALYZING DURATIONS   95

same techniques, due to the type of processes being analyzed. The states of interest are seldom life and death, and, although for example getting a divorce may be conceptualized in terms of failing to maintain a relationship (or, indeed, a personal failure), the term 'failure time-analysis' would seem largely inappropriate as well.

In the remainder of this chapter these techniques will be referred to as survival analysis. We first treat the basic concepts used in survival analysis (the survival function and the hazard rate). We then distinguish between continuous-time and discrete-time survival analysis, and discuss several techniques suitable for the analysis of such data.

Survival data

Survival data consist of sequences of qualitative states to which the participants belonged during a particular period, information on the timing of transitions from one state to another, and (usually) the scores for additional variables, often measured at discrete time intervals. For example, Figure 6.1 shows what might be called a person's 'relational career'. The person in Figure 6.1 was married at the start of the observation period (t_0), but, after three time units, s/he separated from their partner and became single. Four time units later, the person apparently found a new partner and moved to the state 'living together'. Their unmarried union lasted for three more time units, after which a marriage followed. This state was not left before the observation period ended; thus, it is likely that this marriage extended beyond t_{12}.

The period between two changes of state or position (for instance, from 'being married' to 'being single') is called an *episode*, *waiting time*, or *spell*. The change from one spell to another is commonly termed a *transition* or (terminal) *event*. Events are denoted by a qualitative (discrete) variable; the states of this variable should be exhaustive and mutually exclusive. Thus, in the example given in Figure 6.1, the person experienced two episodes of

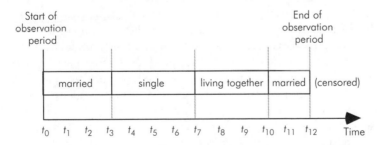

Figure 6.1   *Development across time of a hypothetical relation career: three states, twelve occasions*

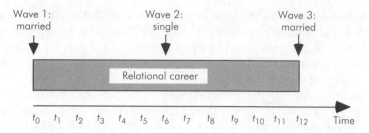

Figure 6.2   *Course of a hypothetical relation career: discrete-time sampling design*

being married, one spell of being single, and one episode of living together with a partner. Three transitions occurred during the observed period (from 'being married' to 'being single'; from 'being single' to 'living together'; and from 'living together' to 'being married'). Further, note that not all beginnings and/or endings of all episodes were observed during the observed period. Such spells are *censored*. For example, in Figure 6.1 the end of the second episode of being married is not observed; this spell is *right-censored*. The beginning of the first episode of being married lies before the start of the observation period, hence, this spell is *left-censored*.

Imagine that a discrete-time instead of a continuous-time sampling design was used to map this person's relational career – for example, by measuring their scores every six time units. Then we would only know the person's scores at t_0, t_6, and t_{12} (Figure 6.2). Comparison of Figures 6.2 and 6.1 shows that employing a discrete-time sampling design can result in a major loss of information. Not only the information on the timing of transitions from one state to another is omitted; investigators may even completely miss out on some of the states the participants belonged to. For example, Figure 6.2 leaves us guessing whether this person experienced an episode of cohabitation before the second episode of being married, or that this person got married immediately.

The risk of failing to detect particular episodes depends on two related factors. One is the spacing between the waves of the study. Obviously, the risk of missing out on relevant transitions is larger if there is a two-year interval between two consecutive waves of the study than if a six-month interval is used. The other factor is the speed at which a particular process develops itself. If many relevant transitions can be expected to occur within a relatively short interval, investigators will miss out on many of these if there is a long interval between the waves of the study. In such cases they are well advised to employ a design with many waves and short intervals between these. (Note that the timing of transitions can often be measured rather well by means of retrospective questions. In such cases the need to conduct follow-up waves at a very frequent rate is less pressing, see Chapter 1.)

Discrete time versus continuous time survival data

In survival analysis it is assumed that information on the timing of the transitions occurred is available. Thus, the exact moment of occurrence of a particular event should be known to the investigator. This raises the question as to *how precisely* the occurrence of an event should be recorded: irrespective of whether time is measured in years, months, days, or seconds, it is always possible to record the event of interest in an even smaller time unit (for example, tenths of seconds, milliseconds, and so on). Thus, the *exact* moment of occurrence of an event is not always known to the investigator. Fortunately, this is not really necessary: what matters is that the course of the process of interest has been recorded in a time unit that is sufficiently small – that is, the data should represent the course of the process in the smallest relevant time unit, given the nature of the process.

The above implies that the choice for a particular time unit should not be a more or less mechanical decision, but should rather be justified on substantial grounds. For example, the durations of employment spells may well be measured in months, as these usually start at the first and terminate at the last day of a month. Similarly, it makes little sense to record the duration of a pregnancy with hour-for-hour precision, whereas months would seem too crude a time unit. Measuring the duration of being pregnant in weeks or – preferably – days would seem more appropriate. Long et al. (1979) focused on the development of academic careers across time. They used rather crude time intervals, namely years, because most academic job changes occur at the beginning of the academic year.

Recording the development of a process in a time unit that is too crude means that relevant information concerning the process may remain unnoticed, which may lead to biased and/or imprecise results. On the other hand, using too small a time unit is not sensible either: the gain in information, compared with that obtained with a more crude time unit, may be limited or even completely absent – whereas the collection of the data may become unnecessarily complex and expensive. For example, if transitions usually occur on a monthly rate, it is unnecessary to use day-for-day precision. If the course of the process of interest is measured in a time unit that matches the nature of this process, the resulting data are said to be measured in continuous time. If time is *not* measured in continuous time, employing a smaller time unit would result in a substantial increase in information.

The data matrix in survival analysis

Continuous-time data may be represented in several ways. Probably the most exotic way to represent survival data to date has been proposed by

Johanson (1987, 1991), who used musical notation to indicate transitions and durations in event histories (a transition from being single to being married – crescendo!). Although this way of representing data is certainly inventive, it is usually more practical to use a 'standard' method to record and code survival data. Such methods often focus on the separate spells that constitute a particular event history. For instance, Karweit and Kertzer's (1986) 'event files' consist of several records per participant, one per event. Each record contains the values of variables at the moment an event occurred; the records are per participant arranged in temporally ascending order. Participants may contribute two or more records (events) to the data set; the fact that these records were contributed by the same participant is often neglected during the analysis.

A second variation on this theme is the 'spell file' (Blossfeld et al., 1989, call this an 'event oriented file'). Again, such files consist of several records per participant. Here the number of records per participant is equal to the number of spells in the event history of this participant. Spell files are very similar to event files, with the important difference that the duration of the spell is added to each record in the spell file.

A third member of this species is Yamaguchi's 'person-age file' (Yamaguchi, 1991; Allison, 1982, codes his data in a similar way); he proposes to construct separate records for each time unit that a person is at risk of experiencing an event. For example, if one uses years as time intervals and the duration of a particular employment spell is five years, five records would be added to the data file. Four of these would contain the information that one time unit was spent being employed; the fifth record would add that this employment spell was over by the end of the fifth unit. This way of coding the data is most useful when dealing with discrete-time data (see below).

It is important not to be confused by the different ways in which survival data can be represented. The differences between the approaches are small when it comes to analyzing the data. Hence, the choice for a particular approach is usually contingent on the expertise and software that is available; the software packages commonly used in the social and behavioral sciences (SAS, BMDP and SPSS) work best with event-oriented files.

Continuous-time survival analysis: hazard function and survival function

The basic kind of data in survival analysis consists of information relating to the duration of belonging to a specific kind of qualitative state, for instance being unemployed or married, living at the parental home, and the like. Survival analysis focuses on the length of these spells, together with a variable signifying whether the end of the episode has been observed (thus, whether a transition to another state has been observed; if not, the spell is right-censored, see Figure 6.1). The values of all relevant explanatory variables at the beginning of each spell are assumed to be known.

A spell is defined as the length of the time interval between two successive transitions. For example, if there are five months between the moment a person was fired and the moment s/he took on another job, the duration of this particular unemployment spell is five months. Assume that we have information on the unemployment spells of a sample of unemployed. Some participants will only be unemployed for a short while, while others need considerably more time to find a job. Indeed, it is possible that some participants have not yet found a job before the end of the observation period. Other participants may drop out before the end of the study; the only thing we know for such participants is that they had not yet found a job at the moment they dropped out – which may be valuable information in itself.

The *hazard rate* λ_t can somewhat loosely be defined as the probability that the event of interest occurs in the time interval $[t, t+\Delta_t]$, provided that this event has not occurred before t. That is, the duration T must be at least equal to t. The hazard rate is not really a probability, as it can be larger than 1; however, for illustrative purposes it is useful to conceptualize the hazard as a chance. Statistically, the hazard rate can be expressed as

$$\lambda_t = \lim_{\Delta\downarrow0} \frac{P(t \leq T \leq t + \Delta t | T \geq t)}{\Delta t} \tag{6.1}$$

Thus, the hazard rate expresses the probability P that the event of interest occurs in the time interval $[t, t+\Delta_t]$, given that the observed duration T is at least equal to t. In continuous-time survival analysis, Δ_t is taken infinitesimally small, which is in equation (6.1) denoted by letting Δ_t approach zero (as in $\Delta\downarrow0$). The arrow indicates that Δ_t is infinitesimally small, but still positive.

The *survival function* S_t expresses the probability that a participant has *not* yet experienced the event of interest as a function of time. It is formally defined as $S_t = P(T > t)$, which gives the proportion of the original population whose survival time T is larger than t (participants who experienced an event are excluded from the sample after time t). The proportion of participants remaining in the sample after time t is often called the 'risk set' – that is, the proportion of the original sample that is still at risk of experiencing a particular event after time point t has elapsed.

The relationship between the survival function and the hazard function can be understood intuitively. Given a specific known hazard function and assuming that episodes only end because of events, the survival function is completely specified. For every interval $[t, t+\Delta_t]$ the size of the population

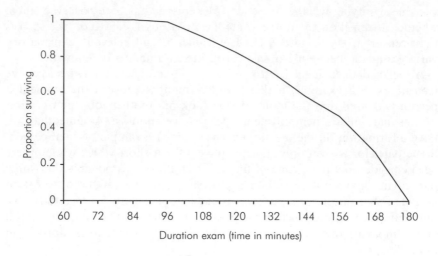

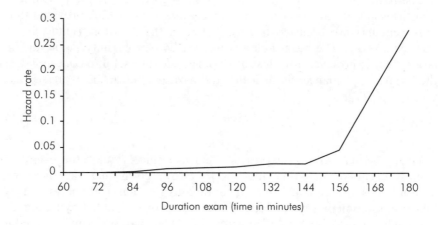

Figure 6.3   *Students handing in their scripts during a statistics exam:*
survival function (top) and hazard function (bottom)

that is at risk at time t can be estimated. It is known from the hazard
function which part of the risk set will experience an event, and how many
participants will survive after time $t + \Delta_t$. Hence, the progression of a
process through time is fully specified by the hazard function.

Example. The concepts introduced above can be clarified by means of a
small example featuring the students of one of the author's former statistics
classes. The variable of interest is the time the students needed to complete
the final exam of this course – that is, the amount of time elapsed (in
minutes) between the moment they were given the questions and the

moment they handed in their answers. The participants had three hours to complete the exam, but they could hand in their answers earlier if they wanted to. No one completed the exam within the first hour; for simplicity 60 minutes were subtracted from all durations. Figure 6.3 presents the resulting survival function and the corresponding hazard function.

As Figure 6.3 shows, the number of students still working on the exam decreases strongly with time. After 84 minutes, almost everyone is still working on the exam; after 120 minutes, about 80 per cent of the students is still busy (20 per cent has already handed in their scripts; in our terminology, they have experienced the event of interest), and so on. No student 'survives' the 180th minute, as they had only three hours to complete the exam. The corresponding hazard rate shows that the probability that the students handed in their scripts increased strongly across time, especially after the 156th minute of the exam.

It is worth noting that whereas the survival function cannot be an increasing function of time, the hazard function can. Indeed, the hazard function may take on very different shapes, dependent on the type of process that is being studied. For example, the chances that women experience a first childbirth is zero for the first twelve years of their lives, then increases strongly, only to become zero again around age 45. Sometimes the hazard rate is a constant across time (in that case, the survival function decreases linearly across time), but this function may also increase or decrease with time, or its path may be wholly unpredictable. This issue is further elaborated later in this chapter.

Right-censored observations   It is possible to analyze duration data by means of analysis of variance or regression analysis, as long as the durations are not right-censored: after all, the duration of such censored episodes is unknown. This implies that such observations yield missing data using these standard techniques. Of course, an investigator might apply any of the strategies to handle missing data discussed in Chapter 2, or discard such observations altogether. However, it is quite likely that this will introduce at least some (and often much, depending on the number of censored observations) amount of error in the analysis.

Obviously, right-censored episodes contain information about the incidence of events, just like uncensored episodes do – namely, censored episodes tell the researcher that the event of interest did not occur before the participant dropped out of the study. In survival analysis, censored episodes are used to compute the hazard function and survival function up to the instant of censoring; subsequently, the episodes are removed from the risk set. Thus, survival analysis uses the information that the event of interest has not yet occurred to a particular censored observation, up to the point at which this observation is censored – a very efficient way to use all information in the data indeed.

Analysis of covariates: the stratification approach

So far, this chapter has been concerned with a discussion of the basic concepts used in survival analysis. We now turn to a more complex issue, namely the analysis of the effects of covariates or explanatory variables. One convenient approach to examine the effects of other variables on the duration variables in the analysis is to divide a sample into several sub-samples (that is, to 'stratify' the sample, for example, on the basis of gender, race, age, and so on), after which for each subsample a separate survival analysis is performed. Comparison of the resulting survival curves then provides an indication of the magnitude of the effects of the covariates. All major statistical packages include a wide range of test statistics that allow investigators to examine whether two or more survival curves are statistically different from each other. Given the aim and scope of this text, it is impossible (and, indeed, unnecessary) to discuss these: interested readers are referred to specialized texts, such as Elandt-Johnson and Johnson (1980).

As an example of this approach, consider a study by Taris and Feij (1997) on the timing of leaving full-time education as a function of historical circumstances. They expected that people would leave full-time education in times of economic recession later than in times of favorable economic circumstances, for two reasons. First, many participants will prefer attending school to just being unemployed. As it will be difficult to find a job in times of recession, many people will simply stay at school in such circumstances. This has the added advantage that more schooling will increase one's chances on the labor market.

Taris and Feij tested this general principle in the context of a longitudinal study on the educational and vocational careers of Dutch youth in the 1980–1990 period. At the beginning of the 1980s, a severe economic crisis hit the world, with youth unemployment sky-rocketing to levels unseen before. People who entered the labor market at that time were sure to be unemployed for a long period. At the middle and end of that decade, however, economic circumstances became much more favorable. Taris and Feij examined the experiences of the members of three birth cohorts: 1961, 1965, and 1969. Members of cohort 1961 were expected to attend school for a relatively long period, as this group would be about to leave school when the economic crisis was at its height (1981). This would especially apply to those with only lower education, as many of these would enter the labor market around that period; members of birth cohort 1961 with a higher education would attend school for another period of time.

Consistent with this reasoning, Taris and Feij created six birth cohort / level of education groups. The survival curves for each group are presented in Figure 6.4. Note that in this case the duration of attending school is identical to age. For example, a person might leave school at age 21; thus,

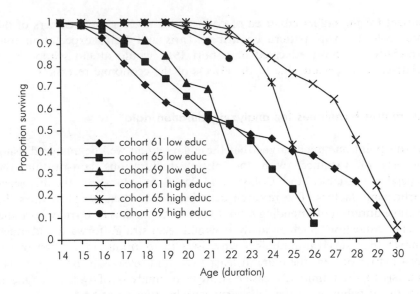

Figure 6.4   *Survival curves for three birth cohorts, low/high level of education*

s/he needed 21 years to complete his or her education. In other cases, however, this need not be the case. For instance, assuming that all participants completed their primary education at age 12 (as is usually the case), we might have taken the number of years the participants needed to complete their secondary education as our dependent variable. In that case, although they would have been linearly dependent, 'age' and 'duration' would not have been identical to each other. Also note that 'age at leaving full-time education' may be measured in a cross-sectional study; again, this presents an instance of a non-longitudinal design yielding longitudinal data (see Chapter 1).

Inspection of Figure 6.4 (and of the corresponding tests, which are not reported here) revealed 'main effects' of Level of education and Birth cohort. As regards the first effect, participants attending lower education needed less time to complete their education than participants attending higher education. Relevant to the main effect of Birth cohort, comparison of the survival curves across birth cohorts showed that each successive birth cohort needed less time to complete a particular level of education than the preceding cohorts.

Further, consider the survival curve for low education for members of cohort 1961. Initially, the members of this cohort seem to leave school earlier than later cohorts. However, at age 20 (that is, in 1981, when the effects of the recession became rapidly visible) the decrease of the survival curve became much slower, up until age 27. Such a pattern was neither present for the higher educated of cohort 1961 nor for the members of the later cohorts. This pattern confirmed Taris and Feij's expectation that especially the lower educated of cohort 1961 would attend school for a relatively long period, due to the effects of the economic recession.

Alternative techniques for analyzing duration data

At this point one might argue that these data could well be analyzed using analysis of variance, with the observed durations constituting the dependent variable, and Cohort and Level of education the between-participants factors. The research question would then be: How does the average duration of attending school vary as a function of birth cohort and level of education? Such an analysis would seem straightforward and much simpler than survival analysis – why use that technique in the first place? As a matter of fact, there are at least two good reasons to prefer survival analysis to the admittedly easier strategy of analysis of variance. One is that the distribution of the dependent variable (the durations) varies across cohort / level of education combinations. The variance of the duration variable is in the youngest cohort clearly much smaller than in the older cohorts, as the highest observed value for the youngest cohort is much lower (namely, age 22) than for the oldest category (which was followed until age 30). Thus, the assumption of homogeneous variances would probably be violated here, meaning that analysis of variance is not appropriate here.

The other reason for preferring survival analysis to analysis of variance is that the participants belonging to the youngest birth cohort often had not yet completed their education at the moment when the data collection phase in this study ended. That is, it is unknown when they will stop attending education; thus, these participants have a missing value for the dependent variable. Omitting these participants would result in a major loss of information and inflated results. *Of course* one will find that members of the youngest birth cohort on average attended school for a shorter period than members of the oldest cohort; after all, the members of the youngest birth cohort who attended school beyond age 22 were explicitly omitted from the analysis! In contrast, the beauty of survival analysis is that it uses all available information. The survival curves of birth cohorts 1961, 1965 and 1969 are compared up to the point that there are no data left for cohort 1969; after that, only the curves of birth cohorts 1965 and 1961 are compared, until none of the members of cohort 1965 has a valid value for duration (that is, after age 26). Similar problems apply when the data are analyzed using regression analysis rather than analysis of variance. Clearly, analysis of duration data by techniques other than survival analysis may yield major problems.

Comparing survival curves

Pairwise comparison of survival (or hazard) functions for different groups is a simple way to examine the differences among the survival times obtained for these groups. Unfortunately, this approach rapidly becomes impractical when the number of survival curves (groups) to be compared increases. For example, the six-group survival analysis in the example above already involved (5 + 4 + 3 + 2 + 1 equals) 15 comparisons (plus one additional overall-test). Further, if a particular sample is divided into many smaller subgroups, the power of the statistical tests (the degree to which a test is able to detect differences among the survival curves of the groups) decreases accordingly; the smaller the size of the groups involved, the lower the chances that the differences between these groups are statistically significant.

Taken together, these problems imply that the simple stratification approach falls short when it comes to controlling the effects of more than just one or two covariates. Indeed, the stratification approach is a far cry from the sophisticated procedures used in – say – regression analysis, where many covariates can be analyzed simultaneously. It is unlikely that the research questions addressed using survival analysis are any less complicated than those for which regression analysis is employed, and this applies even more if the study goes beyond a straightforward comparison of two groups that differ systematically on just a single experimental variable. In such cases additional variables must be included in the analysis to avoid the results being virtually meaningless, as they are confounded with the effects of uncontrolled variables. Therefore, since the early 1970s statisticians have attempted to develop survival models that can handle many covariates in a flexible manner. Some of these are discussed in the next section.

Parametric and semi-parametric approaches to analyzing covariates

The dependent variable in survival analysis is the likelihood (or hazard) that an observation will terminate as a result of the occurrence of a particular event of interest. Consider the model

$$\lambda(t) = \lambda_0(t)\exp(\beta z), \tag{6.2}$$

in which the hazard $\lambda(t)$ at time t is a function of a 'baseline' hazard function $\lambda_0(t)$, and the effects of the p covariates (these are in the $p \times 1$ vector of covariates z, with the corresponding effect parameters in vector β). The function $\lambda_0(t)$ contains a particular standard distribution of the hazard rate across time, and the basic shape of this function is the same for all participants. Further, the risk of a terminal event is also dependent on the participants' scores on the covariates in vector z: for some participants the chances of experiencing an event are larger or smaller than for others, due to their combination of scores on the covariates.

The regression approach to survival analysis discussed below comes in two basic variations. In the first, investigators must specify a particular a priori parametric distribution for the shape of $\lambda_0(t)$. Alternatively, $\lambda_0(t)$ may be left unspecified, in which case a semi-parametric model is obtained without any assumptions concerning the shape of the baseline hazard function.

Modeling the hazard function: parametric approaches

In parametric models the hazard function is assumed to comply with a particular functional distribution. For instance, the hazard may be believed to be the same at all time points (a constant); in that case the hazard rate is 'exponentially' distributed. In other cases the hazard rate is assumed to vary over time. For instance, McGinnis (1968) proposed that the chances that employees will leave their job decrease over time due to 'cumulative inertia'. As people invest in their jobs, build up a social network, attend job-specific training programs, and so forth, it will become increasingly difficult for them to leave their jobs. The basic shape of the hazard function $\lambda_0(t)$ can be specified accordingly as a decreasing function of time. In other instances, the hazard function may be believed to decrease (increase) in an early stage of the process, and to increase (decrease) only after some time has elapsed. And so on: there are many other, more or less sophisticated and/or complicated, ways to specify the hazard function (see Blossfeld et al., 1989, or Hutchison, 1988a, 1988b, for overviews).

It is important to choose the 'right' functional distribution of the hazard rate $\lambda_0(t)$, because the estimates of the effects of the explanatory variables are estimated in relation to (thus, they are dependent on) the distribution being chosen. Thus, an erroneous specification may lead to biased parameter estimates. Unfortunately, as the proper functional form is seldom known to the investigator, choosing the correct distribution is a difficult issue, especially since people tend to disagree as regards the right shape of the hazard rate. For example, while McGinnis (1968) contended that the risk of leaving a job would decrease across time, Nicholson (1987) argued that people would become *more* likely to leave a job as time proceeds, as they will get tired of going through the same routine every day. In the presence of such contradictory expectations, investigators may either want to examine what the proper specification of the hazard rate is (a research question that might be interesting in its own right), or use techniques that do not require them to specify a functional distribution. As in many instances investigators are not particularly interested in the distribution of the baseline hazard function but rather in the effects of the covariates, they often opt for a *semi*-parametric model.

The semi-parametric survival model

The semi-parametric model developed by Cox (1972, 1975) is often more appropriate than a parametric model. The Cox model does not assume any specific distributional shape for the baseline hazard function $\lambda_0(t)$. This is useful when the investigator does not have explicit ideas about the shape of this function, when the hazard rate is too irregular to fit any particular distribution, or when one is only interested in the magnitude and direction of the effects of the explanatory variables. As Hutchison argued, 'The semi-parametric approach is of particular value in the social sciences, where there is barely any reason to assume a particular functional form' (1988a: 214), while Yamaguchi (1991: 76) emphasized that, unless the investigator intends to test specific hypotheses regarding the shape of the hazard rate, '. . . a parametric characterization of time dependence is not recommended'.

Cox (1972) gives the model

$$\lambda(t|z) = \exp(z\beta)\lambda_0(t), \tag{6.3}$$

in which z is a vector of p covariates, β a $p \times 1$ vector of parameter estimates and $\lambda_0(t)$ an unknown function giving the hazard function for an unspecified baseline model – that is, $z = 0$. It is assumed that the ratio of the hazard for any two individuals – controlling for all covariates – is constant, and does not depend on time. Stated differently, the hazard rates for each pair of individuals must be proportional at all times; consequently, this model is also denoted as the 'proportional hazards' model.

Time-varying covariates Another attractive feature of the semi-parametric model is that time-varying covariates (explanatory variables, the values of which may change across time) can easily be included in the analysis. Imagine that an investigator sets out to examine the effects of childbirth on women's employment careers. S/he may start off with a sample of women who are with or without child at the start of the observed period. A simple approach to examine the effects of having a baby on the employment career would be to estimate a model in which employment status at time t is regressed on the employment status at time $t-1$ and the family status at time $t-1$ (family status indicating whether the woman has a child). Figure 6.5(a) presents a graphical representation of this discrete-time design. This model addresses the question whether the presence of a child at time $t-1$ predicts women's employment status at time t, controlling employment status at time $t-1$.

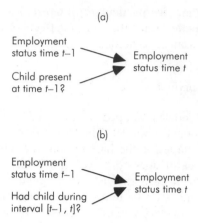

Figure 6.5 · *Examination of effects of having a baby on women's employment: (a) discrete-time model; (b) semi-dynamic model*

This simple approach does not hold water, however, as it neglects the fact that women may have their first child during the interval $[t-1, t]$; this is not reflected in their time $t-1$ score, but may certainly affect their employment status at time t. The model presented in Figure 6.5(a) may be modified to account for this problem, by replacing time $t-1$ Family status with a variable that indicates whether women had their first baby during the interval $[t-1, t]$, as in Figure 6.5(b). Obviously, model 6.5(b) can only be fitted for women who were without child at $t-1$. In effect, model 6.5(b) examines whether having a first baby during the interval $[t-1, t]$ predicts women's employment status at time t, controlling their employment status at $t-1$.

Trivial as it may seem, a semi-dynamic model such as 6.5(b) differs from a truly dynamic model in that the timing of changes regarding the dependent variable (a change of employment status) and the explanatory variables (a change of family status) are neglected. This implies that potentially important information about the order of changes in these variables may be lost. Given this discrete-time design, it is impossible to distinguish a woman who leaves the labor market first and then has a baby from a woman who first has a baby and then leaves the labor market, if these changes all occur within the interval $[t-1, t]$. The discrete-time semi-dynamic approach may not detect such differences, which could lead to biased results (e.g., Raffalovich and Knoke, 1983; Sandefur and Tuma, 1987).

Thus, we would like to fit a dynamic model in which the timing of change in the covariates is taken into account. One such model is the hazard function

$$\lambda(t|x(t)) = \exp(x(t)\beta)\lambda_0(t). \tag{6.4}$$

As can be seen from equation 6.4, the values of the covariate vector x are considered to be varying across time. Let covariate $x_i(t)$ be a dummy variable that indicates whether person i belongs to state A or state B at time t. If the participant belongs to state A, $x_i(t)$ becomes 0; if the participant belongs to B, $x_i(t)$ equals 1. Now, the value of $x_i(t)$ may change in time. For instance, if the data to be analyzed concern the duration of having a specific job, $x_i(t)$ might be a variable indicating whether this person has children. The value of $x_i(t)$ should change accordingly; only then can the parameter estimates in vector β be estimated properly. Although this may sound rather complicated, this is a matter of routine in most of the standard software packages that perform proportional hazards survival analysis (such as BMDP and SAS). For more information about the incorporation of time-varying explanatory variables see Blossfeld et al. (1989), Blossfeld and Röhwer (1995), and Petersen (1986); the latter discusses the incorporation of time-varying covariates in the context of parametric models.

Handling error in survival models   As you may have noted, equations 6.2–6.4 only model the effects of the variables that were included in the model. However, other variables may affect the course of the hazard rate as well. For example, a model may be misspecified, in that important explanatory variables were omitted or not measured at all. In the common linear regression models this problem is solved by introducing a *disturbance* or *error term* in the equation, representing the effects of the variables that were not included in the model. We know that in regression analysis the effects of variables are biased when important explanatory variables that correlate with the variables in the model are not controlled. Further, the variance of the parameters of the model will be overestimated, leading to overly conservative tests of the significance of these. Similar results can be expected in the case of survival models (Andress, 1989). For example, let a sample consist of people who belong to either group A or group B. The hazard rate is constant over time for both groups, but members of group B have a much lower chance to experience the event of interest than members of group A. Failing to control for group membership would then result in a hazard rate that declines across time, as the members of group A experience the event of interest rather soon, while many members of group B will still be in the sample (compare Chapter 2, in which a decreasing likelihood to drop out of the study signified that wave nonresponse was selective). Clearly, misspecification of the model may result in erroneous conclusions regarding the shape of the hazard rate, and this may have more or less severe implications for the estimates of the effects included in the model. Therefore, since the middle of the 1980s efforts have been made to extend the survival model with an error term (Andress, 1989; Heckman and Singer, 1984; Trussell and Richards, 1985).

In practice, the extension of a survival model with an error term often means that the original distribution of the durations is combined with a particular distribution for the disturbances, the shape of which must a priori be specified by the investigator. It is already difficult to choose the 'right' functional distribution for the hazard rate (as must be done in parametric survival analysis); it is even harder to think of a suitable distribution for the error term. Further, as yet it is unclear whether inclusion of an error term really improves parameter estimates; after the promising results initially reported by Heckman and Singer (1984), follow-up studies have repeatedly shown that parameter estimates remained biased, whether or not the models examined in these studies included an error term. Although some investigators attribute these disappointing results to an erroneous choice of the distribution of the error terms, Andress (1989) showed that even Heckman and Singer's (1984) non-parametric (or distribution-free) approach led to biased results. He therefore concludes that '. . . there is no easy way out of the specification problem, at least not by statistical procedures. Even models with miscellaneous error distributions [models that do not assume a parametric distribution for the shape of the error term – TWT] do not yield better estimates . . . The best solution seems to be better substantial theories and more extensive and precise data' (1989: 22). The specification problem can therefore not be resolved by statistical means; it is up to the investigator to specify models that include all relevant variables.

Competing risks analysis The last topic to be addressed here is what is known as *competing risks analysis* (Hachen, 1988). Consider a study concerning the life course of people who have been diagnosed as being carriers of the AIDS-virus. These people have a high risk of death from consequences of AIDS. However, rather than dying from AIDS-related diseases, these people may be killed in a traffic accident or commit suicide instead; such non-AIDS related events in effect also remove the person from the risk set. It is often the case that episodes can be terminated by several, qualitatively different, events; once one of these has occurred, the participant is not at risk of experiencing any of the other events. One might say that these events 'compete' to terminate the episode, and only one of them can be the winner.

Statistically, the event-specific hazard rate may be written as

$$\lambda_{t,j} = \lim_{\Delta \downarrow 0} \frac{P(t \leq T \leq t + \Delta t, Y = j | T \geq t)}{\Delta t}, \quad (6.5)$$

where Y is a state variable with J ($j = 1, \ldots, J$) categories. These categories correspond with the terminal events under consideration. As in equation 6.1, equation 6.5 is the limit of the probability that an individual experiences a transition during the time interval $[t,t+\Delta t]$, given that up to time t no transition has occurred; however, now only the transition to state j is of interest. The overall hazard rate at time t is simply the sum of all transition specific hazard rates (Allison, 1984; Blossfeld et al., 1989; Elandt-Johnson and Johnson, 1980).

It is quite possible that not all J events are of interest to the investigator. For example, only the AIDS-related events will be of interest in the AIDS-study mentioned above. In this case, the episodes terminating due to non-AIDS-related events can be considered as being right-censored. Thus, in the analysis it is taken into account that the participant did not die because of AIDS until censoring occurred.

Alternatively, the investigator may consider *all* types of terminal events of substantive interest. For example, in a study on job turnover, several possibly important (and theoretically interesting) terminal events may be conceived. Workers may leave their current employer for another employer; they may have a similar or a better job there. A worker may have been fired. Finally, a worker may leave the labor force altogether, for example, due to retirement. It is very likely that different causal processes underlie these events. For example, the last terminal event (retirement) will probably be largely accounted for by age, whereas leaving a particular job for a similar job elsewhere may be due to an unpleasant relation with one's direct chief or co-workers and little commitment to the organization, but also to personal circumstances (e.g., one has found a partner who lives elsewhere). And so forth; for each type of terminal event a different set of possible antecedents and causes can be construed.

Failing to discriminate among these distinct types of events (by treating them as basically similar events by classifying them in the same category) may well lead to results that cannot be interpreted. For example, the explanatory variables may actually affect one kind of event, but not the others; they may increase the chances of occurrence of one type of event, while decreasing the chances of occurrence of another event, and so on. To prevent this type of problem, it is imperative that investigators consider a priori the types of events that are relevant given the process that is examined. Obviously, these events must be analyzed separately in the analysis phase.

Competing risks analysis is conceptually different from the situation in which there are two or more events that can in principle remove an observation from the risk set, but where the process that determines the timing of such a removal is the same for both events. For example, assume that a researcher is interested in the time it takes for a consumer to buy a new car. There are many cars to choose from. If one purchases a Toyota, one ceases to be at risk of buying a Ford or a Buick (at least for some time to come). That is, the purchase of a car of a particular make terminates the state of being at risk of buying a car of another make, and in this sense the analysis of the purchase of a car presents an instance of a competing risks analysis. However, the crucial difference is that the purchase of a new car may best be conceptualized as a *two-step process*. In the first step the consumer decides that it is time to buy a new car; in the second step, the buyer decides *which* car will be bought.

The first part of this process can be studied using survival analysis, by relating the time during which one drove the old car to the characteristics of this car (such as mileage, make, and number of seats), characteristics of the driver (e.g., wealth, socio-economic class, family status, gender), and so forth. The second part of the process can be analyzed using multinomial logit analysis (a statistical technique in which the dependent variable is categorical), in which the purchase of a *particular* make of car is related to other variables. Thus, here it is assumed that the process that determines the time it takes before one decides to buy a new car is the same, *irrespective of the make of the car one buys*. In competing risks analysis, however, it is assumed that this process is dependent upon the outcome of the process – that is, that a different causal process may be at work for each outcome.

Example: continuity of women's employment after childbirth

One common finding is that women tend to adjust the number of hours they work after they have a baby. They often leave the labor market, giving up employment in order to have more time to take care of the increased household chores. However, they may also take up part-time employment; this option increases the time that they can spend on their household as well. It might well be that the causal structure that underlies these two options is qualitatively different: whereas leaving the labor market is a very traditional choice that is probably heavily influenced by religious and traditionalist values, taking up part-time employment may be considered to be a more rational choice. Therefore, there seems some reason to study a transition towards part-time employment in its own right, rather than to consider it as just a derivative of leaving the labor market.

Table 6.1 presents the results of a competing risks analysis of the factors that determine the course of the employment career of young women after having a baby. Among these are job characteristics (job level, number of hours worked, amount of labor market experience), background variables (level of education, birth cohort, partner status), and attitudinal variables (male/female traditionalism). Note that the scores on partner status and whether there is a small child present may vary across time, as can the interaction effects involving these variables. Table 6.1 shows that the causal processes underlying the choice for either option differ strongly. Whereas the decision to leave the labor market is mainly contingent on whether the woman has a child (in combination with, to some degree, the presence of a

Table 6.1 *Parameter estimates of full and final equations (significant effects only) for a semi-parametric competing risks survival analysis of the course of the employment career of employed women*

| | Event of interest | | | |
| | Leave labor market | | Work part-time | |
Variables	Full equation	Significant effects only	Full equation	Significant effects only
Cohort 1961 versus cohorts 1965/69	-.63		-1.30**	-1.00**
Religious commitment	.06		.23	
Partner present[1]	.10*		-.03	
Level of education	-.10		.04	
Job level	.60		-3.34**	-2.72**
Number of hours worked	.01		.09**	.08**
Year entry labor market	.01	.01*	-.01	
Child present[1]	3.48	6.99**	3.10**	2.84**
Child present × M/F traditionalism[1]	-.85	-.86*	-.35	
Child present × partner present[1]	-.25**	-.27**	-.02	
Child present × job level[1]	1.59		6.10**	4.82*
L^2 (df)	180.4 (11)	178.4 (4)	96.9 (11)	67.6 (5)
p (L^2)	.00	.00	.00	.00

* $p < .05$, ** $p < .01$.
[1] Time-varying covariate.

partner and male/female role orientation), job level is a major determinant of taking up part-time employment after childbirth. The significant Presence child × Job level interaction effect suggests that job level is a major determinant of taking up part-time employment after the birth of the first child; this effect was not significant for the first analysis (leaving the labor market).

Continuous-time survival analysis: evaluation and discussion

Up until now, this chapter has been concerned with several forms of continuous-time survival analysis. Versatile and useful as these approaches may be, they also have some drawbacks. The parametric approaches assume a particular functional distribution of the hazard function; as the shape of this distribution is often unknown to the investigator, this assumption may be violated in everyday research. This problem is overcome by the semi-parametric model, but this approach has the disadvantage that it assumes that the hazard function has the same basic shape for every observation (proportional hazards). The ratio of the hazard for any two participants must be a constant and should not be dependent on time. This assumption can be tested using several tests (Blossfeld et al., 1989), which amount to specifying an interaction between time (duration) and the covariates. If this interaction is significant, this assumption of the proportional hazards model is violated, and other techniques (for example, parametric models) should be employed instead.

The approaches discussed above assume that time has been measured continuously; they are 'continuous-time' approaches. Continuous-time techniques assume that the n observed survival times T_i ($i = 1, 2, \ldots, n$) can be unambiguously ordered according to duration and, thus, that no two survival times are of equal length; there are no 'ties' in the data. However, even if the course of the process of interest has been recorded in continuous time, there may be many ties in the data. If so, it may be better to turn to discrete-time survival techniques. This topic is discussed below.

Discrete-time survival analysis

There may be important reasons to choose another mode of analysis than the continuous-time survival techniques considered in this chapter. The assumption that durations are measured in continuous time may not be realistic, there may be many ties in the data, or the investigator may suspect that the proportionality assumption of the semi-parametric model is violated. In such cases it is often useful to turn to the discrete-time variant of survival analysis. The remainder of this chapter therefore discusses a frequently used mode of discrete-time survival analysis.

Assume that the duration of belonging to a particular state has not been measured in continuous time, but in a cruder time unit. For example, the duration of employment spells has been measured in three-month rather than in one-month intervals. Employing the continuous-time approach would be rather cumbersome here, as there will be many tied durations (these cannot be ordered unambiguously, as many persons will have left their jobs within the same three-month episode). Thus, application of continuous-time survival analysis is not appropriate. Fortunately, there are methods that can analyze such discrete-time data; indeed, these may even be easier to apply than their continuous-time counterparts.

Allison (1982, 1984) gives the discrete-time hazard rate

$$P_{it} = Pr\ (T_i = t | T_t \geq t,\ x_{it}),\qquad(6.6)$$

where x_{it} is a vector of covariates, and T is the discrete variable giving the uncensored time of event occurrence. It is also the conditional probability that an event occurs at time t, given that it has not occurred before t. The relation between the discrete-time hazard rate and the explanatory variables is given by

$$P_{it} = \frac{1}{1 + \exp(-\alpha_i - \beta x_{it})}.\qquad(6.7a)$$

Written in logit form, equation 6.7a becomes

$$\log \frac{P_{it}}{1 - P_{it}} = \alpha_t + \beta x_{it}. \tag{6.7b}$$

According to equation 6.7b, the logit of the probability that an event occurs at time t, given that it has not yet occurred, depends on a constant α_t and a set of covariates in x_{it}, weighted by a set of parameter values β. As α_t is usually left unspecified, equation 6.7b is the discrete-time analog of the Cox (1972) proportional hazards model given in equation 6.3.

How can we estimate a model such as equation 6.7b? Allison (1982) proposes the following procedure. Let the maximum observed duration in this example be seven units (of for instance twelve months), and assume for simplicity that the values of the covariates are constant across time, and that only one transition is of interest (that is, no competing risks here). This data set can be used to create seven separate sub-data sets, each corresponding with one of the seven observed time units. The first sub-data set would include the scores of all participants on the covariates, as well as a variable indicating whether the transition of interest has occurred during the first interval. The second sub-data set would consist of all participants that had not experienced the event of interest by the end of the first time unit (the risk set at the start of time 2). Again, the values of the covariates would be included in this sub-data set, as well as the dichotomous variable indicating the occurrence of the event of interest. And so on: the seventh data set consists of the scores of all participants that had not experienced the event of interest at the end of the sixth time unit, and the dichotomous variable indicating whether the event of interest occurred during the seventh interval.

Participants who do not experience the event of interest during the seven observed time units contribute one record to all seven data sets, while people who experience the event of interest in, say, the second time unit contribute two records to only two data sets. Right-censored observations can be included in the data sets, up until the moment censoring takes place. Finally, all seven data sets are pooled, resulting in one large data set. The pooled data set is then analyzed by means of standard logistic regression analysis, with the dependent variable being the variable indicating whether the event of interest occurred during a particular time unit.

Note that most of the participants will contribute more than a single episode to the pooled data set, which means that the observations in the pooled data set are not statistically independent. Thus, the assumption of many standard statistical techniques (including regression analysis and analysis of variance) that the observations in the data set are statistically independent is violated. However, if the fitted model given in equation 6.7b is an exact representation of the process at hand (if *all* individual variance in the hazard rate is captured or 'explained' by the explanatory variables), the maximum likelihood-estimates will remain consistent, asymptotically efficient, and asymptotically normally distributed (Allison, 1982). In such cases the observations in the pooled data set can be analyzed as if they were statistically independent. However, if the model does not include all relevant variables (which will often be the case), the consequences are uncertain. A correct specification would then be

$$\log \frac{P_{it}}{1 - P_{it}} = \alpha_t + \beta x_{it} + \varepsilon_{it}, \tag{6.8}$$

where model 6.7b is extended with an error term ε_{it}. If model 6.8 is correct, estimation of a model without an error term will probably yield biased parameter estimates. A complication arises from the fact that the error terms for each individual will usually be correlated over time; the error in the hazard rate will therefore have some across-time stability. By analogy with ordinary least-squares regression analysis, this would lead us to expect that standard errors under 6.7b will be inflated, thus rejecting the null hypothesis of no effect too often.

Example: the transition towards non-virginity

This example focuses on the factors that affect the timing of the transition towards non-virginity. 255 English adolescents aged between 13 and 18 years were interviewed twice with regard to their sexual behavior (in 1989 and 1990, respectively). Among the variables being measured were gender, parental socio-economic status, adolescent attitudes towards having sex (sexual permissiveness, importance attached to knowing their partner before having sex with them, and importance attached to loving the partner before having sex with them), and courtship behaviors. With regard to the latter variables, the participants had to estimate the degree to which they thought it likely that they would perform a variety of behaviors if they were to meet an attractive member of the opposite sex, after having danced the whole evening with this person and knowing that the other person feels very attracted to them as well. Factor analysis revealed a stable two-factor structure, with rather innocent courtship behaviors such as 'holding hands together' and 'share a drink together' loading on this factor. The second factor involved rather less innocent courtship behaviors, among which were 'trying to have intercourse without a condom' and 'masturbate each other'. Taris and Semin (1997) provide full details on the operationalization of the variables and the design of the study.

The 255 participants were asked to indicate whether they had had sexual intercourse, and, if so, how old they were when this first happened. 102 participants said that they had already had intercourse before the first wave of the study. Another 55 participants became sexually experienced during

Table 6.2   Results of a discrete-time survival analysis concerning the factors that determine the timing of the transition towards non-virginity

	Full equation	Significant effects only
Gender (high = male)	-.34*	-.32*
Socio-economic status of parents	.09	
Sexual permissiveness	.13	
Importance of loving the partner before agreeing to have intercourse	-1.81**	-2.19**
Importance of knowing partner well before agreeing to have intercourse	-.08	
Courtship behavior: 'innocent' behaviors	-.14	
Courtship behavior: other behaviors	.05	
Constant	-2.41	-.71

* $p < .05$, ** $p < .001$.

the observed period. The remainder of the sample did not experience the transition to non-virginhood before the end of the observation period.

Following the procedure outlined above, several different data sets were created. The first data set contained data on all 255 participants. This data set included a variable indicating whether the participant was still a virgin as a 13-year old, as well as the scores on the explanatory variables. The second data set included only those participants who were still virgin as a 13-year old ($n = 253$). This data set included a variable indicating whether the participant was still a virgin as a 14-year old, together with the participants' scores on the explanatory variables at the first wave of the study, and so on. The seventh (and final) data set included all participants that were still virgins as 18-year olds. Subsequently the seven data sets were pooled. This led to a data set consisting of no less than 1,225 year-person episodes, 157 of which were terminated by an event. The other 1,068 episodes were right-censored.

The data set was analyzed using logistic regression analysis. Table 6.2 presents the results of this analysis. Boys experience the transition towards non-virginhood somewhat later than girls; and adolescents who feel that loving the partner is important in order to have sex with them experience their first intercourse later than others (a very significant –2.19). The other variables are not significant.

Concluding remarks

The present chapter discussed methods suitable for analyzing duration data. These methods use the available information regarding the course of a particular process more efficiently than other longitudinal methods, such as the discrete-time two-wave panel model (for example, Raffalovich and Knoke, 1983; Sandefur and Tuma, 1987). However, the methods presented here suffer from a number of drawbacks. First, they require a fair amount of data manipulation, and the data must sometimes be analyzed using rather user-unfriendly software (although this problem has largely been resolved since the introduction of Windows-versions of the major statistical packages). Second, investigators must choose a suitable model for the data. If a parametric survival model is chosen, the question remains which specification of the hazard function is correct. As regards the semi-parametric approach, the assumption of proportional hazards may not be satisfied. Neither the fully nor the semi-parametric methods are well suited for the analysis of competing-risks models; a separate analysis must be conducted for each type of event.

Further, the approaches discussed in this chapter are more or less of limited use, as the values of the covariates are assumed to be known over the whole duration of the episode. This means that in practice only covariates whose value changes very little across time can be included (such as gender, age, socio-economic status, job level, and the like), apart from other variables that were measured in continuous time. If this assumption is not satisfied, the parameter estimates will become dependent on the length of the period under study, and will not improve upon the results of the discrete-time methods presented in Chapter 4.

Further reading

The current chapter provided a basic introduction to the analysis of duration data. We have discussed the approaches that are likely to be of most interest to social and behavioral scientists. However, there are several other, slightly different approaches that may also be of some importance to researchers. Survival analysis as discussed in this chapter is a mathematically quite sophisticated way of analyzing the life-tables that have been used in demography and actuarial science since the end of the 19th century. Such life-tables are simply a survival function presented in the form of a table. That is, these tables show the risk that a particular observation is still at risk of experiencing a terminal event at a number of discrete time intervals. A standard textbook on this matter has been written by Pollard et al. (1981). The virtue of this text is that it provides many examples of how the life-table approach can be used to answer very specific research questions that may be of interest to investigators. Elandt-Johnson and Johnson (1980) provide a statistically much more thorough review of the life-table approach. Their book is strongly recommended for those who want to make the most of their life-table analyses. Both texts provide the reader with a wealth of examples and exercises.

A simple introduction to continuous-time survival analysis can be found in Allison (1984). Slightly more sophisticated introductions are provided by

Blossfeld et al. (1989), Blossfeld and Röhwer (1995), Parmar and Machin (1995), and Yamaguchi (1991). The latter text is of special interest to investigators who are interested in discrete-time approaches to survival analysis, as is Vermunt (1997), who provides an excellent discussion of the application of log-linear models to event history analysis, with special attention to the problem of missing values. Finally, Cox and Oakes (1984) and Tuma and Hannan (1984) provide mathematically sophisticated reviews of survival analysis. However, these texts are rather abstract and therefore less appropriate for those who are just starting to develop an interest in these methods.

7   Analyzing Sequences

Event history data consist of sequences of qualitatively different states occupied by the participants during the observation period, as well as the timing of transitions from one state to another. Such data can be analyzed by focusing on the occurrence of particular approaches (as was done in Chapter 6), but also by examining event histories *as wholes*. This chapter presents several approaches to characterizing the course of event histories. First I discuss the use of simple indexes (representing the number of transitions, the nature of these, and/or their uncommonness). I then address methods for devising classifications of careers.

Event- vs career-centered modes of analysis

The previous chapter addressed a by now well-known approach to the analysis of event history data. As regards the analysis of such data, it is convenient to distinguish between event-centered and career-centered methods. In *event-centered modes of analysis*, the investigator focuses on the occurrence of particular types of events – for example, a transition from employment to unemployment, from married to single, etc. Two typical instances of event-centered methods are survival analysis (which was discussed in the previous chapter) and discrete-time regression methods (in which the dependent variable represents the occurrence of a particular transition during a particular period; such methods were discussed in Chapter 4).

Although the event-centered approach is relatively simple and conceptually unambiguous (results can easily be related to substantive research questions, typically questions like 'what determines the occurrence of transition X?'), the fact that event histories usually consist of more than a single transition is usually neglected. This is unfortunate, as it may well be theoretically important to examine the course of the career as a whole, rather than as a more or less random sequence of presumedly isolated events or states.

Due to the growing awareness that there is more to the analysis of event histories than survival analysis only, over the last decade or so other approaches to the analysis of event history data have attracted a good deal of attention, especially due to the work of Abbott and his co-workers

(Abbott and Barman, 1997; Abbott and Hrycak, 1990). Rather than studying particular episodes of an event history or the determinants of a specific transition, such *career-centered modes of analysis* focus on the classification of event histories taken as wholes. Their goal is to characterize the development of (parts of) event histories. Several transitions may occur within this time period, and these are all in some form included in the analysis. Typically, this mode of analysis results in classifications of career trajectories. Such classifications may be linked to explanatory variables, resulting in an analysis of the determinants of a particular *career* type, rather than of a particular *transition* type.

One of the big issues in this tradition is how the number of distinct careers can be reduced to a manageable number. If careers are observed at eight occasions and participants can belong to one out of four states, the number of distinct careers already amounts to 8^4 (as many as 4,096 careers)! Clearly, reduction of the number of careers is imperative in this approach. The current chapter reviews some of the more feasible of these. The first part of this chapter deals with simple indexes that characterize the course of careers during a particular interval. These indexes highlight different aspects of career development; some focus on the amount of change, others on the degree to which there is upward or downward change, yet others on the uncommonness of particular changes (Taris and Feij, 1999). The second part of this chapter reviews methods for creating career classifications.

Measuring career change: characterizing development

Generally speaking, measures of career change differ with respect to two dimensions, namely whether these measures are (partly) based on evaluative judgements about the nature of transitions (valence; for example, there may be 'good' vs 'bad', or 'upward' vs 'downward' transitions), and whether they focus on the absolute vs the relative amount of change. As regards the valence of transitions, some approaches do not distinguish among different types of transitions. As an example we mention the common practice in vocational psychology of measuring job turnover in terms of a dichotomous variable that indicates whether a person has found another job. It is, however, often sensible to distinguish between voluntary or involuntary (or: downward vs upward) transitions, as involuntary job changes may be linked to very different sets of antecedents and consequences than voluntary job changes.

This distinction may be subject to criticism insofar as it involves subjective judgements about the nature of particular transitions. Investigators usually need an external criterion to judge the valence of a particular transition: why is a particular transition considered positive or negative? As the choice of such a criterion depends on the theoretical framework adopted for the study, it may be subject to criticism. For example, a transition to a higher-level job (usually a positive transition) often brings about increased work stress and lower well-being. Thus, from a different point of view, this transition might well be considered negative.

Absolute vs relative amount of change. It is often convenient to focus on the absolute amount of change in a career trajectory – that is, to count the number of transitions that have occurred (possibly with constraints on the type of transitions that are of interest). The amount of change $C(x)$ in a particular career trajectory x may be computed as

$$C(x) = \left(\sum_{t_{ijx}} |t_{ij} \in T \right) \tag{7.1}$$

where t_{ij} indicates a transition from state s_i at time i to state s_j at time j, and T the pool of transition types that are of interest. Obviously, the meaning of $C(x)$ depends on the definition of T. For example, if T includes all transitions in a particular career trajectory, $C(x)$ indicates the amount of change in a career. However, if T is defined as the pool of positive (negative) transitions, $C(x)$ may be taken as an indicator of upward (downward) mobility – although it is probably better to devise an indicator in which positive (upward) transitions and negative (downward) transitions may *compensate* each other. For instance, if a particular career trajectory includes two positive transitions followed by five negative transitions, it seems unreasonable to speak of a generally 'upward' employment career, as the number of downward transitions exceeds the number of upward transitions.

This way of measuring change simply tells us what *is* – that is, how often particular events occur in a career trajectory; we do not know how a particular career compares to other careers. However, this issue may be of considerable interest. For example, Spencer and McCall define '. . . order-disorder [. . .] as the extent to which the career approximates the normative pattern implied in a career line for the number and timing of job changes. If a given manager is late in making a particular job transition that many of his or her counterpart managers have made by the same age, then there is some degree of disorder because the career departs from the career line' (1982: 22). Thus, what matters here is not so much *whether* a manager has made a particular transition or *how many* transitions s/he has experienced, but rather how a particular transition fits in with the normative (or average) career trajectory that applies for managers in this particular organization. This line of reasoning suggests that one potentially fruitful conceptualization of career mobility examines the degree to which particular transitions are 'common' or 'uncommon', relative to the careers of comparable others.

One approach to measuring the uncommonness of a particular career trajectory is to compute the relative uncommonness of the transitions included in this trajectory. An often-occurring transition would receive a low weight, while a transition that occurs only rarely would be weighted heavily (Abbott and Hrycak, 1990, propose a similar approach). The uncommonness UNC(x) of a career trajectory x can then be computed as

$$\text{UNC}(x) = (\textstyle\sum_i \sum_j t_{ijx} \; w_{ij} | t_{ij} \in T), \tag{7.2}$$

where t_{ij} is the number of transitions of state s_i at time i to state s_j at time j, and w_{ij} is the weight associated with this transition. Abbott and Hrycak (1990) suggest weighting the transitions t_{ij} by their relative frequency of occurrence. This approach to constructing weights is based on the information in the careers themselves; no subjective judgements of the valence of events are needed. Hence, the methodological problems regarding the application of an external criterion do not apply. Evaluations of particular events can be included, however, by assigning the appropriate sign to the weights w_{ij}.

Illustration: sensation seeking, job characteristics and mobility

The notions discussed above are illustrated in a four-year longitudinal study on the effects of a personality construct (two scales of Zuckerman's, 1994, sensation-seeking construct) on the career mobility of employed young Dutch adults. Being a sensation seeker may have implications for the development of one's employment career. For example, sensation seekers will feel bored more quickly than others, and it can be assumed that they will tend to change jobs more often than others. Further, particular pathological manifestations of the sensation-seeking trait (such as impulsive personality disorders, antisocial tendencies, excessive use of alcohol, substance abuse, and absenteeism) may interfere with work behavior and career development.

In examining the effects of sensation seeking on the development of the employment career, investigators may focus on very different aspects of career development. First, they may emphasize *absolute* change – sensation seekers will experience more change than others. They may also consider *relative* change – sensation seekers will experience more uncommon transitions than others. Further, sensation seekers might experience relatively many *negative* transitions (transitions to a lower-level job, long-term unemployment), as substance abuse, absenteeism and the like tend to affect the employer–employee relationship.

Participants were 357 employed Dutch adults who were all born in 1961. At both waves of the study (which was conducted in 1987/88 and 1991/92), information was collected about the number, nature and timing of changes regarding their employment careers. This allowed us to create a precise record of the course of events on these domains. The six mobility indexes were created on the basis of the information presented in Table 7.1.

Table 7.1   Description of the construction of the career indexes

Transitions	(1) X	(2) Total freq.	(3) Valence	(4) Relative frequency of occurrence (x)	(5) Weight (1/x)	(6) Weight × valence
(1) < 2 months unemployed	1.16	515	+	.60	1.67	1.67
(2) 3–11 months unemployed	.41	208	–	.24	4.17	–4.17
(3) ≥ 12 months unemployed	1.06	134	–	.16	6.25	–6.25
Total		857				
(4) Higher-level job	.67	215	+	.25	4.00	4.00
(5) Same-level job	1.59	519	+	.61	1.64	1.64
(6) Lower-level job	.38	123	–	.14	7.14	–7.14
Total		857				

Each transition towards a new job yielded two separate pieces of information. One of these pertained to the *length of the unemployment episode* separating two jobs. We distinguished among (very) short, moderately long, and long unemployment spells (events 1 to 3 in Table 7.1). Moderately long (3–11 months) and long unemployment spells (more than 12 months) were considered negative events (column 4 in Table 7.1), whereas a (very) short unemployment spell (less than 2 months) was considered a positive event. The other piece of information concerned the *level of the new job*, compared with the previous job. One could experience a transition towards a higher-level, same-level, or lower-level job (events 4 to 6). As Table 7.1 shows, finding a same-level or higher-level job was considered a positive event; a transition towards a lower-level job was considered negative.

Further, Table 7.1 presents: the average rate of occurrence of each transition per career trajectory (column 1); the number of times a particular transition occurred (summed across all career trajectories, column 2); the relative rate of occurrence (x) of each particular episode – that is, the frequency presented in column 2 divided by the total number of empirically occurring transitions (857); the weight associated with each transition (following Abbott and Hrycak, 1990, computed as $1/x$, column 5); and weight times the valence of the transition (column 6). For instance, our participants contributed 857 transitions in total. Of these, 134 (16 per cent) were preceded by a period of long-term unemployment. Multiplication of this proportion by $1/x$ yields a weight of 6.25, meaning that experiencing a period of long-term unemployment is quite uncommon.

Six indexes were computed from this information. Four of these were based on the absolute frequency of occurrence of (particular sets of) transitions, whereas the remaining two emphasized the relative frequency of occurrence of the transitions. For each participant, the *total number of transitions* (TnT) was computed using equation 7.1. As the focus is on the total number of transitions, T includes *all* transitions included in a particular participant's event history (see Table 7.1). Thus, TnT is a simple measure of the absolute amount of change in a particular career trajectory.

T can be constrained to include only positive or negative transitions. The *total number of positive transitions* (TnP) was computed using equation 7.1, but now the pool of transitions of interest T only included the positive transitions in Table 7.1. In a similar vein, equation 7.1 was used to compute the *total number of negative transitions* (TnN), by letting T include only negative transitions. TnP and TnN might be considered indexes that represent the amount of upward (downward) mobility that a particular career trajectory contains. As noted earlier, a good indicator of upward (downward) career mobility requires that upward and downward transitions are allowed to 'compensate' each other. Thus, a fourth index *Career Progression* (CPR) was computed as the number of positive transitions TnP minus the number of negative transitions TnN. CPR represents the overall progression of the career during the observed interval, in that positive and negative events may compensate each other. As such, it is a better measure of upward (downward) career mobility than either TnP or TnN.

The *uncommonness* (UNC) of the career trajectories was computed using equation 7.2. The transitions t_{ij} were weighted by their relative frequency of occurrence. First we constructed a transition matrix that presented the likelihood of a transition from state s_i to state s_j, irrespective of the timing of these transitions. The proportions in the transition matrix were then turned into weights by taking their inverse $1/x$, yielding a weight matrix in which frequently occurring transitions received low weights, whereas uncommon transitions received large weights (Table 7.1).

Finally, appropriate signs were assigned to the weights derived for the mean uncommonness of a career, yielding the Weighted Career Progression (WCP). For example, the uncommonness of a transition from employment to a lower level job was 7.14; this particular transition was considered negative. Hence, the contribution of any such transition to the weighted mean progression of a career was −7.14.

This study featured two scales of the sensation-seeking construct: *Disinhibition*, with typical items like 'I feel good after a couple of drinks', and 'I like wild parties', and *Boredom Susceptibility*, including items such as 'I lose interest quickly if people or things around me remain the same', and 'I would like to have a job requiring traveling around the world'. The scores on these scales were taken as indicators of a latent trait 'sensation seeking'. The other explanatory variables included in this analysis were permanency of the participants' first job, the level of that job, the participants' level of education, their amount of labor market experience (time elapsed since they took on their first job), and gender. The data were analyzed using covariance structure modeling (Jöreskog and Sörbom, 1993). For simplicity all explanatory variables were assumed to affect all six mobility indexes. After

Table 7.2   Standardized Maximum Likelihood estimates for the final model

Variables	TnT	TnP	TnN	CPR	UNC	WCP
Sensation seeking[1]	.13**	.13**	.08**	.10**	.14**	
Gender (hi = male)	-.08*	-.10*		-.10*	-.06*	-.08*
Labor market experience	.17**	.11**	.22**		.22**	-.16**
Level of education						.12**
Level first job						-.13**
Appointment type (hi = permanent)	-.25**	-.24**	-.17**	-.17**	-.22**	
R^2	.07	.05	.10	.04	.06	.37

NB: TnT = total number of transitions, TnP = total number of positive transitions, TnN = total number of negative transitions, CPR = career progression, UNC = uncommonness career, WCP = weighted mean career progression.
[1] Latent variable, loading of Disinhibition was .64 ($p < .01$), loading of Boredom susceptibility was fixed for identification purposes.
* $p < .05$, ** $p < .01$.

omitting the non-significant effects, a final model was obtained with a chi-square value of 34.59 with 27 df, $p > .10$. Table 7.2 presents the estimates for this model, showing that the pattern of effects of the explanatory variables was very similar for five out of the six mobility indexes. For example, sensation seekers were likely to experience both many positive (TnP) and many negative events (TnN), resulting in a career trajectory that contained significantly more transitions than the careers of others (TnT). Further, there was a positive effect of sensation seeking on the difference between the number of positive and the number of negative events (CPR), suggesting that sensation seekers experienced more upward mobility than others. Finally, sensation seekers experienced relatively uncommon events, as evidenced by the positive effect of sensation seeking on the uncommonness of the career (UNC). The other effects can be interpreted in a similar fashion.

Despite the strong similarity of the pattern of effects for TnT, TnP, TnN, CPR and UNC, it must be noted that there were also several important differences among the indexes. For example, gender affected all mobility indexes, with the notable exception of the number of negative events that occurred in a particular career trajectory. Also note that the strength of effects tends to vary across different mobility measures. Despite these differences, these five mobility indexes all seem to work in a similar way. This is probably due to the fact that positive events occurred far more frequently than negative events, leading the first to 'overwhelm' the latter. It is likely that results would have been rather different, were the number of positive and negative events to have been more equal.

For the sixth index (the Weighted mean Career Progression WCP), a very different pattern of effects was obtained. Most interestingly, whereas sensation seekers seemed to experience more upward career mobility than others, this effect disappeared when the uncommonness of the transitions was taken into account. Further, we found effects of level of education and of the level of the first job that were not obtained for the other five indexes. Clearly, WCP measures a rather different concept than the other five indexes.

Evaluation   This section presented six indexes highlighting different aspects of the course of careers. Some of these emphasize the absolute amount of change that occurred during a particular time interval (frequency), whereas others focus on the amount of change, relative to other careers (uncommonness). Further, we distinguished between approaches that involved an evaluation of the nature of particular transitions, vs approaches that considered all transitions equal. An example in which all six indexes were applied revealed that the patterns of results obtained for these indexes may be quite similar, especially if particular transitions occur far more frequently than other events. However, it should be noted that despite such empirical similarities, the theoretical meanings of the indexes presented here are rather different. That is, the choice for either of these indexes should be based on theoretical considerations.

Creating classifications of careers: distance-based methods

The mobility indexes presented above focused on the type and number of transitions that occurred during the event histories of the participants, resulting in a quantification of the careers of interest (in terms of amount of mobility, uncommonness, etc.). Another approach focuses on classifications of similar careers. One common strategy is to classify the careers on the basis of the order of occurrence of the transitions constituting these careers. For example, Hogan (1978) classified his data on the basis of the six logically possible orders of the three events of interest. This strategy is feasible only if the sequences contain a limited number of elements, so that there are only few combinations possible. Hogan accomplished this by ignoring the time dimension in his data, focusing on the order of the events of interest only. Yet, the timing of particular transitions (thus, the time the participants spend in the states of interest) may constitute a very important difference between two in other respects identical career trajectories. For example, consider two career trajectories that were observed for eight occasions in time:

1   A B C C C C C C
2   A A A B B B C C

Both trajectories follow the same basic pattern of transitions (one transition from A to B, followed by a transition from B to C). Were the time dimension to be ignored, then both sequences would be of the form [A B

C]. However, these two sequences differ strongly regarding the timing of the transitions. In trajectory 1 the transitions occurred in an early stage of the career, whereas in trajectory 2 the transitions are more or less equally spaced across the career. The timing of their transitions may indicate a theoretically important distinction between these careers. For example, trajectory 1 may represent the career of a once-promising young employee (a 'high-potential') whose career got bogged down for some reason, whereas trajectory 2 is the 'standard' career pattern for that organization. If it is the case that the future development of a career depends strongly on its past development (as proposed in, for example, Rosenbaum's (1979) tournament model), employee 2 may well experience a promotion shortly; conversely, it seems time for employee 1 to seek a job elsewhere.

Neither the mobility indexes presented above nor Hogan's (1978) enumeration procedure will detect the subtle, yet important differences between career trajectories 1 and 2. Therefore, other strategies are needed to create viable classifications of event histories. This section addresses two such approaches in some depth. Both share the feature that they group event histories on the basis of a distance matrix – that is, a symmetric $n \times n$ matrix, with n being the number of event histories. For each pair of event histories a number representing the difference (or distance) between these is computed. This number is then entered at the appropriate place in the distance matrix.

A distance matrix is in some respects much like an ordinary correlation matrix. However, whereas the off-diagonal elements in a correlation matrix represent the strength of the association between pairs of variables (or, perhaps, their similarity; correlations can be interpreted as reflecting the degree to which two variables are the same, Hubert, 1979), the off-diagonal elements in a distance matrix denote the difference between pairs of sequences (or event histories). Just like a correlation matrix, a distance matrix can be used as the input for further analysis. For example, distance matrixes are routinely analyzed by means of cluster analysis, yielding groups (or 'clusters') of participants who resemble each other strongly (as evidenced by low distance scores). These clusters can then be linked to other variables. In this vein, investigators can examine whether male and female employees follow different career paths, whether past career influences future career development, and so on.

One important issue in this approach is the choice of a particular distance measure. There are many ways of computing the distance between two careers. The remainder of this chapter addresses two distinct approaches, which are both more or less exemplary for a broader class of similar approaches. The approaches belonging to one of these classes compute distances on the basis of what may be labeled a 'same-time, same-state' (STSS) principle. An alternative class of approaches focuses on the order of the states occupied by the participants ('same-order' (SO) approaches).

Table 7.3   *Three hypothetical careers for 10 occasions*

Time:	1	2	3	4	5	6	7	8	9	10
Tom	A	A	A	B	C	D	D	D	E	F
Dick	A	A	A	A	A	D	D	E	F	F
Harry	A	B	B	B	C	C	D	E	E	E

Same-time, same-state methods: correspondence analysis of careers

The basic assumption of STSS approaches is that the careers of persons who belonged to the same states at particular moments in time are more similar than the careers of persons who belonged to different states at these moments. STSS approaches consider particular 'slices' of time and check to which state the participants belong. If two persons belong to the same state at the slice of time under consideration, the distance between the careers of these persons does not increase. Conversely, if they are in different states, the distance does increase. Consider as an example the careers of Tom, Dick, and Harry presented in Table 7.3. At time 1 they are all in the same state; thus, this time point is not very helpful in distinguishing among their careers. However, for times 2 and 3 we find that Harry is in a different state from Tom and Dick, meaning that the distance between Harry on the one hand and Tom and Dick on the other increases. As Tom and Dick are in the same state at the first three time points, the distance between their careers is zero after three time points. However, at time 4 Tom has moved to state B, whereas Dick and Harry remain in the same state as at time 3. Now Tom and Harry are in the same state, and Dick is the one who differs from the two others. And so forth.

After 10 time points, Tom and Dick have shared the same states for 6 time points (thus, the distance between Tom and Dick may be said to be 4 points); Tom and Harry belonged to the same states for 5 time points (distance Tom vs Harry: 5 points); and Dick and Harry occupied the same states for only 3 time points (distance Dick vs Harry: 7 points). These distances can be presented graphically in a two-dimensional space, as in Figure 7.1.

Note that, in principle, $n-1$ dimensions are needed to represent the distances among n observations. Thus, to represent the distances among two careers, only one dimension is needed; two dimensions are needed for three careers; three dimensions for four careers; and so on. Figure 7.1 suggests that Tom and Dick's careers are relatively similar, whereas Harry's career is relatively far removed from the other two careers. Thus, it seems reasonable to assume that if two classes of careers are to be created and the number of differences is the criterion for computing distances,

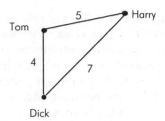

Figure 7.1   *Representation of the distances among Tom, Dick and Harry's careers*

Tom and Dick's careers would fall into one class of careers, whereas Harry's would fall into the other.

Of course, if there are only three careers it is quite easy to detect the similarities and differences among these, even if we only have tables presenting raw career data (such as Table 7.3). However, this soon becomes impossible when the number of careers to be compared increases. This is where statistical procedures such as cluster analysis become exceedingly helpful. Simply stated, cluster analysis first computes a distance matrix, then forms groups of similar cases in a stepwise fashion. Eventually, cluster analysis will combine classes of similar cases with other classes of similar cases, until all cases fall into the same class. It is up to the investigator to decide at which point it is no longer meaningful to combine classes of careers with other classes.

At first sight, cluster analysis seems a rather simple and therefore attractive approach for arriving at a limited number of distinct classes of careers. However, one important problem in this approach is that cluster analysis was devised as a tool for grouping cases on the basis of their scores on interval-level variables. However, the states in our event histories are *qualitatively different* from each other. As such, they cannot directly be analyzed using cluster analysis. The traditional solution to the problem of including qualitative variables in statistical procedures devised for the analysis of interval-level variables is to create *dummy variables*. The process of creating dummy variables is essentially one of turning qualitative variables into quantitative variables: for every category of a quantitative variable a new variable is created. As dummy variables take on a value of 0 or 1, they can be included in procedures devised for interval-level variables like any other interval-level variable. For example, if a particular nominal variable has two categories (say, gender: male vs female), two dummy variables could be created. On the 'male' variable, women would receive the score 0 and men the score 1; on the 'female' variable, men would receive the score 0 and women the score 1. Obviously, if the score on the 'female' variable is known, the score on the 'male' variable is known as well and vice versa. Therefore, one of the dummy variables must be omitted from the analysis.

The same principle applies when the variable of interest has more than two categories. For example, Claes et al. (1992) used cluster analysis to create a classification of the career patterns of young workers in eight countries. They distinguished among eight qualitative states to which the participants could belong (such as 'employed', 'unemployed', and 'attending school') at either of eight time points. For each time point they created seven dummy variables indicating whether the participant belonged to either of the corresponding states. Only then were the resulting 7 (states) × 8 (occasions) variables subjected to the cluster analysis – a laborious procedure indeed, and not one to be recommended, as many statistical packages now include a procedure that is much better suited for the analysis of nominal career data, namely correspondence (or conjoint) analysis.

Correspondence analysis of career data

Generally speaking, correspondence analysis (CA) is appropriate for the analysis of square two-way cross-tables without negative cell entries. This matrix is approached through a lower-order matrix, allowing the investigator to study the most important aspects of the data in a lower-dimensional space. The rows and columns can be plotted graphically. If two (or more) row (column) points are close to each other, they are similar; if they lie far apart, they differ strongly. In fact, the output of CA consists of graphical representations of the distances among row (column) points. Like Figure 7.1, visual inspection of the plots of row (column) points provided by CA may already yield considerable understanding of the data structure. On the basis of these plots, investigators may decide about the number of clusters that should be distinguished, the internal consistency of these clusters, and which observations should be assigned to a particular cluster.

Career data can also be represented in a two-dimensional table, with the rows representing the sequences of states occupied by the participants and the columns representing the time points at which the participants occupied particular states. This approach, which was first proposed by Saporta (1981) and Deville and Saporta (1983), and was refined by Van der Heijden and his colleagues (Van der Heijden and De Leeuw, 1989; Van der Heijden et al., 1997), is an easy-to-use and flexible tool for creating career classifications. As many readers will be unfamiliar with CA, below we discuss its basics in somewhat more detail.

Principles of correspondence analysis   Consider a data matrix consisting of five persons and four columns (Table 7.4(a)). The columns represent four different states, say, 'employed', 'unemployed', 'not available for the labor market', and 'other', respectively. The cells of this table contain the number of weeks a person spent in any of these states during an observation period

Table 7.4   *Event history data for five persons across a two-year interval*

| Persons | (a) Number of weeks spent in four states | | | | | (b) Proportion of weeks spent in four states | | | | |
	f	g	h	i	Total	f	g	h	i	Total
a	0	40	12	52	104	.00	.38	.12	.50	1.00
b	14	10	40	40	104	.13	.10	.38	.38	1.00
c	0	0	24	80	104	.00	.00	.23	.77	1.00
d	70	17	17	0	104	.67	.16	.16	.00	1.00
e	42	10	10	42	104	.40	.00	.10	.40	1.00
Total	126	77	103	214		.24	.15	.20	.41	

NB: f = 'employed', g = 'unemployed', h = 'not available for the labor market', i = 'other'.

of two years. For example, person a was not employed during the observed period, spent 40 weeks being unemployed, was not available for the labor market for 12 weeks, and was in the 'other' category for 52 weeks.

When comparing the event histories of these five persons, investigators may consider the proportions of time spent in each of the four states. These proportions are given in Table 7.4(b). This table shows that the event history of person a resembles that of person c, at least in terms of the number of weeks spent in the four states of interest; the careers of persons b, d, and e are rather different from a and c's careers.

Tables as small as Table 7.4 can easily be inspected by eye. However, when the number of states and/or states of interest increases, CA may help the investigator to gain insight into the data. Assume that the interest lies in the comparison of the event histories. Here Table 7.4(b) will probably be of more help, as this table clearly shows how the event histories of the persons are compiled. CA uses this representation of the data as well. There, the five persons are each represented by a single point in a four-dimensional space, with the proportions given in Table 7.4(b) as the coordinates of the persons in this space. Thus, person a is located at (.00, .38, .12, .50), person b at (.13, .10, .38, .38), and so forth. The distances among the persons in this four-dimensional space are indicative of the similarity and differences among their careers: those who have followed a similar career path will be located close to each other, and persons that lie far apart have followed rather different career trajectories.

The 'average' row computed from the five persons has coordinates (.24, .15, .20, .41), and these are identical to the proportions at the bottom line of Table 7.4(b). The difference between the average row (or the origin) and row i indicates the degree to which person i's career deviates from the 'average' career, as computed across all five persons.

Examination of the distances among row points in more than two or three dimensions usually yields little insight into the data. The dimensionality of the solution can be reduced by reconstructing the high-dimensional space in such a way that each subsequent dimension captures as much as possible of

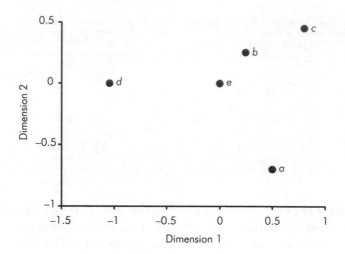

Figure 7.2   *Representation of the distances among the careers of five hypothetical persons*

the distances among the persons in the four-dimensional space. In fact, CA uses the same procedure that is used in ordinary principal components factor analysis; CA is therefore sometimes referred to as 'principal components analysis of categorical data'. Like factor analysis, CA yields eigenvalues that reflect the importance of a particular dimension in 'explaining' the differences among the persons. In the example, the first three eigenvalues are .41, .13, and .05, respectively, and these dimensions explain 67 per cent, 23 per cent, and 6 per cent of the differences among the persons, respectively. Thus, examination of only the first two dimensions of the solution already yields considerable insight into the distances among the careers of the persons.

The corresponding two-dimensional representation of the row points is given in Figure 7.2. This figure shows that the careers of persons b, c, d, and e are all located on a line that roughly parallels the first dimension, and that the second dimension is dominated by persons a and c. Careers b and e resemble each other strongly, as evidenced by a small distance between the corresponding row points. The career of person e is much like the average career, as shown by its location close to the origin (0, 0) of the figure, etc.

Disaggregating the data matrix   Table 7.4 showed data for the course of five careers across two years. This is a fairly long period, meaning that much information about the actual sequence of the states may be lost. For example, person d spent 17 weeks of this period being unemployed, 70 weeks being employed, and 17 weeks being not available for the labor market. However, we know nothing about the order in which person d

passed through these states. It may well be that at the beginning of the observed period person d was employed for 70 weeks, then became unemployed for 17 weeks, only to leave the labor market altogether. However, any other sequence of states may apply equally well, as long as these comply with the numbers presented in Table 7.4. Disaggregation of Table 7.4 into two one-year intervals would already give more information about the order of the states, but nothing withholds the investigator from analyzing a 5 (persons) × 104 (weeks) × 4 (states) matrix. Although in that case we must speak of *multiple* correspondence analysis, the resulting plots can be interpreted as usual. The drawback of extreme disaggregation, however, is that the results may become unstable, especially for small samples.

Finally, it is worth noting that the plots produced by CA provide researchers with graphical information about the distances among the careers of the participants in their sample. These plots can be inspected by eye, yielding information about the number of clusters present in the data. The participants' scores on the dimensions of interest can also be added to the data file as extra variables, presenting interval-level information about the distances between the participants' (qualitative) careers. These interval-level scores can then be further analyzed using cluster analysis. Effectively, this results in a two-step procedure that combines the strengths of both cluster analysis and correspondence analysis, making it a flexible tool for analyzing sequential data.

Example: correspondence analysis of educational and vocational careers   As an example of analyzing sequential career data by means of correspondence analysis, I re-analyze part of the data previously analyzed by Claes et al. (1992). All participants in this study participated in a three-wave, six-nation study on the work socialization of youth (WOSY International Research Group, 1989). At the first wave, the 537 participants included in the current study were asked to indicate what their primary activity had been during the eight three-month intervals preceding the start of the study. Thus, there were eight state variables that corresponded with each of these three-month intervals. In this illustration I focus on four main categories of these variables: regular work (either full time or part time); attending education (either coherent or incoherent with the job the participants held at the first wave of the study); some combination of attending education and working; and other (out of work, military or civil service).

These eight four-state variables were entered into a correspondence analysis. The first five eigenvalues of the solution were .64, .55, .23, .21, and .18, suggesting that limiting the analysis to the first two dimensions only would not result in a major loss of information. Figure 7.3 presents the distances among the participants graphically, showing that there are several clusters of observations in the data. Three of these are more or less

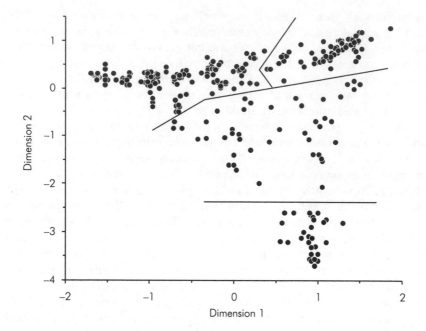

Figure 7.3   *Representation of the distances among the careers of 537 young workers*

well-defined; one in the lower half of the figure, one in the upper right, and one in the upper left. Furthermore, there are several observations in between these clusters. As these do not clearly belong to one of the three well-defined clusters, these may be taken as a fourth cluster.

Note that the observations that are close to the origin (at point (0,0)) strongly resemble the 'average' career pattern. Thus, the careers in the upper half of Figure 7.3 are quite similar to this 'average' career, whereas the careers at the bottom of this figure are rather dissimilar. One way of going about these results is to add the scores of the participants on the two dimensions to the original data file, and analyze these scores by means of cluster analysis. This should yield a typology of four distinct clusters of careers, and understanding of the nature of these clusters (careers) can by obtained by comparison of the scores on the eight state variables across the four clusters.

However, one attractive feature of CA is that it allows for an immediate interpretation of the differences among the participants as well. Up until now, the discussion of CA for the analysis of career data has focused on the distances among the careers of the participants. A very similar analysis can be conducted for the categories of the state variables. Actually, plots of the distances among the categories of the variables used in the analysis are

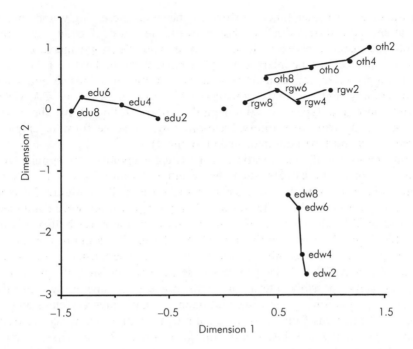

Figure 7.4   Representation of the distances among the categories of the career variables (time points 2, 4, 6, and 8; other time points omitted). NB. 'edu' = full/part-time education; 'rgw' = full/part-time regular work; 'edw' = some combination of work and education; 'oth' = 'other'. The numbers refer to time points

part of the standard output of many programs for doing CA. Figure 7.4 presents the distances among the categories of four of the state variables used in the analysis (namely, for interval 2, 4, 6, and 8; the scores for the other four intervals were also included in the analysis, but not given in this figure, to ease interpretation of the results). Similar categories are connected by straight lines. As Figure 7.4 reveals, the categories of the four state variables form little sequences, the order of which corresponds neatly with the time of measurement.

The origin, representing the 'average' category, is (as always) located at point (0,0). Category points that are close to the origin do not discriminate strongly among the participants; they are quite common, and thus resemble the average category quite strongly. The larger the distance between a particular category point and the origin, the less this category resembles the average category and the more it discriminates among the participants. For example, Figure 7.4 shows that at time 2 is quite common to attend education, as evidenced by the fact that category point edu2 is quite close to the origin. At later times, however, it becomes increasingly uncommon to attend education, which is shown by the location of edu4, edu6 and edu8: the distance between these categories and the origin increases. The other sequences can be interpreted in a similar fashion. That is, it becomes increasingly more common to have a regular job, to combine education with employment, or to be unemployed. Thus, in this way CA yields insight into the typical developmental patterns followed by the participants: away from attending education, towards some form of employment (or, it must be admitted, unemployment).

But this is not all. The location of the category points corresponds with the location of the careers, such that Figures 7.3 and 7.4 can readily be compared. For example, the cluster in the lower half of Figure 7.3 consisted of careers in which education and employment often were combined, as evidenced by the location of these categories in the lower half of Figure 7.4. Similarly, the cluster in the upper left of Figure 7.3 contains the careers of people who were mainly attending education. The cluster in the upper right of Figure 7.3 includes people whose careers consisted of episodes of regular work, possibly alternating with episodes of unemployment (the category points for regular work and unemployment are very close, implying that transitions from work to unemployment and vice versa are quite common). Finally, the cluster in the middle of Figure 7.3 consists of careers in which episodes of attending education, employment and unemployment alternate with each other.

Same-order methods: sequencing careers

Correspondence analysis of event histories is a typical same-time, same-state approach. The basic assumption of such approaches is that careers are more similar when they share more of their states at particular time intervals. Reasonable as this may sound, it is important to note that this mode of analysis completely ignores the order of the elements (states) of the event histories, and that no advantage is taken of the temporal information in the data. This is shown by the fact that the columns in the data matrix (tables such as Table 7.4) can be interchanged, without any consequences for the resulting classification; the distances computed from this data matrix remain the same (Abbott and Hrycak, 1990). Yet, information about the order of the elements in the sequences to be compared may be absolutely essential for obtaining viable career classifications. Consider, for example, the following two careers which were observed for six discrete time points:

A B C D E F
B C D E F G

You will probably agree that both sequences are very similar. Yet, same-time, same-state approaches will consider these sequences as being *completely different*, because they share none of their elements at any given time point! Clearly, something is amiss here; STSS approaches fail to take into account the information about the order of the elements constituting the sequences.

The realization that STSS approaches use only part of the information in the data has led to the development of a rather different class of statistical approaches, that explicitly take into account the order of the states of the sequences to be compared. These are here denoted as 'same-order' (SO) approaches. Below we first address the optimal matching procedure proposed by Abbott and his colleagues (Abbott and Hrycak, 1990; Abbott and Barman, 1997), and then proceed with a discussion of Dijkstra and Taris's (1995) variation on this approach.

Optimal matching of careers. Abbott and his co-workers showed that order is an important issue in the classification of event histories. More-over, they proposed a method to compute distances between pairs of event histories, explicitly taking into account the temporal order of the elements in these careers. This 'optimal matching' approach was originally developed in the biomedical sciences for examining the similarity between DNA and RNA sequences (Doolittle, 1990). Optimal matching involves the computation of the minimum number of alterations necessary to turn a particular sequence into the sequence it is compared to. The more alterations are necessary, the greater the difference (and, hence, the greater the distance) between these sequences. Alterations may be made in either of three ways. First, redundant elements in the first sequence may be omitted. Second, elements of the second sequence that are missing in the first may be inserted at the appropriate places. Third, nonfitting elements in the first sequence may be replaced by an appropriate element. The total number of changes (deletions, insertions, and replacements) needed to obtain a perfect match is taken as an indication of the distance between the two sequences.

In some cases the approach advocated by Abbott yields somewhat unrealistic measures of the similarity of sequences. Consider the following three sequences:

$$A\ A\ A\ E\ F\ G \qquad (1)$$
$$E\ F\ G\ C\ C\ C \qquad (2)$$
$$D\ D\ D\ D\ D\ D \qquad (3)$$

According to the algorithm proposed by Abbott and Hrycak (1990), six changes are needed to turn sequence (1) into sequence (2) (for example, the three As at the beginning of (1) and the three Cs at the end of (3) could be deleted; or the three As of sequence (1) could be omitted, and the sequence E F G might be added to (1), and so forth). However, the distance between sequence (2) and (3) also equals six, just as the distance between (1) and (3).

Hence, according to Abbott's approach, all three sequences are equally dissimilar, despite the fact that sequences (1) and (2) share as many as three elements in the same order. Therefore, rather than discuss Abbott's approach at some length, we describe a slightly different approach that also uses the order of states to compute distances among careers, which was developed by Dijkstra and Taris (1995).

Like the optimal matching procedure proposed by Abbott and Hrycak, the method discussed here is based on the number of transformations needed to turn one sequence into the other. In the first step of this approach, all codes of a sequence that do not occur in the other are removed from both sequences. Take, for example, the sequences

$$A\ C\ E\ B\ A\ D\ E\ F \qquad\qquad (4)$$
$$A\ G\ H\ B\ C\ C\ B\ C\ D\ I \qquad\qquad (5)$$

Codes E and F from sequence (4) do not occur in sequence (5), and are omitted from (4). Similarly, the codes G, H and I from sequence (5) do not return in sequence (4). This step results in the sequences

$$A\ C\ B\ A\ D \qquad\qquad (4a)$$
$$A\ B\ C\ C\ B\ C\ D \qquad\qquad (5a)$$

In the second step, superfluous codes are omitted. For example, there is only one code C in sequence (4a), whereas there are as many as three Cs in sequence (5a), whereas code A occurs twice in sequence (4a) but only once in (5a). The superfluous codes are omitted, until both sequences contain exactly the same codes. The order of these codes, however, may still be different. Note that the choice to omit particular codes from the sequences is *not* a more or less arbitrary one. The superfluous codes are omitted in such a way, that the resulting sequences resemble each other maximally. That is, the number of inversions needed in the next step of the analysis is minimized. For example, one code A had to be omitted from (4a); the A to be omitted is the second A, rather than the first. Similarly, the last two codes C must be omitted from sequence (5a) to obtain an optimal match, not the first. Thus, this step yields the two sequences

$$A\ C\ B\ D \qquad\qquad (4b)$$
$$A\ C\ B\ D \qquad\qquad (5b)$$

The third and final step involves the computation of the number of moves needed to turn sequence (5a) into sequence (5b). In this case, it is sufficient to change the order of codes C and B in either sequence (4b) or (4a) (one move necessary). As the number of moves usually depends on the length of the initial sequences (4) and (5), the number of moves is adjusted for the length of the initial sequences. The resulting distances between pairs of sequences can, again, be used to create a distance matrix, which can be further analyzed by means of cluster analysis.

Table 7.5   States of Living, Education, and Employment

Living	
H	(home, with parents)
S	(single, living alone)
P	(with partner, unmarried)
M	(with partner, married)
O	(other, for example, student dormitory)
Education	
F	(Full-time)
P	(Part-time)
O	(not attending school)
Employment	
F	(Full-time: 5 days a week)
P	(Part-time: 1-4 days a week)
O	(not employed: less than 1 day a week)

As an illustration, Dijkstra and Taris (1995) presented an example concerning the vocational, educational and family careers of 494 participants in a four-year longitudinal study. They distinguished among various states, which are given in Table 7.5. The life history of each respondent can be described as a sequence of distinct states. A transition from one state to another was defined as a change in at least one of the aforementioned variables. An example of such a coded life history is

HF0 SF0 S0F S0F M0F

The first state (HF0) signifies that this respondent lives at home with their parents (H), attends full-time education (F), and is not employed (0). The second state (SF0) shows that this person still attends full-time education and is not employed; however, s/he has left their parents and now lives alone (S for 'single'). The other states can be interpreted similarly.

One way of linking the distances among careers to other variables is by creating clusters of similar careers, much as was done in the preceding section. Another possibility is by finding and comparing the sequences that are typical for particular subgroups. Dijkstra and Taris (1995) distinguished among male and female respondents, and found the following sequences to be the most typical life histories for these two groups:

females: HF0 H00 H0F P0F M0F M00
males: HF0 H00 H0F H00 H0F P0F M0F

Clearly, there are strong similarities between these 'typical' sequences. However, there are also some differences, the most notable being that women tend to leave the labor market after their marriage whereas men do not. Thus, women and men tend to follow rather traditional career paths.

Table 7.6   Average distance between
a traditional life history and actual life
histories as a function of SES

SES	No. of sequences	Mean distance	Variance
0 (low)	4	.36	.04
1	102	.42	.04
2	70	.45	.04
3	95	.48	.04
4	82	.51	.03
5	58	.56	.03
6	43	.60	.03
7	28	.68	.03
8	10	.62	.01
9 (high)	2	.82	.00
Total	494	.50	.04

Investigators may want to examine the antecedents of the choice for a particular career path. For example, is it true that low socio-economic status (SES) is associated with a traditional career path? To examine this issue, Dijkstra and Taris (1995) defined a 'traditional' four-element life history:

$$HF0 \ H00 \ H0F \ M0F$$

Thus, after completing his or her education the respondent finds a job, then leaves home to marry. They then calculated the average distance between this 'traditional' life history and all sequences in their data file within 10 SES classes (Table 7.6). As Table 7.6 reveals, the average distance between the 'traditional' career path and the actual career paths increases with SES: $F(9,484) = 8.39$, $p < .001$. In the lowest SES group the average distance between the actual careers and the traditional career is quite small; in the highest SES group, the average distance is considerably higher.

Further reading

This chapter described methods for characterizing the development of event histories. We distinguished between two typical modes of data analysis. One of these aimed to characterize the development of careers, by focusing on the number, direction and relative frequency of the moves constituting the event histories. The other involved the computation of distances among careers; the resulting distance matrix could then be subjected to a cluster analysis (Everitt, 1981, provides a short but very helpful introduction to the basics of cluster analysis). Distances were computed on the basis of what was called a 'same-state, same-time' principle, using (multiple) correspondence analysis. An accessible introduction to CA is given by Greenacre (1984); a mathematically more sophisticated introduction can be found in Gifi (1990). The second approach to calculating distances was proposed by Abbott and his colleagues. As yet, no accessible standard text for social and behavioral scientists dealing with his optimal matching procedure has been published, but the reader may consult Abbott and Hrycak (1990) and Abbott and Barman (1997) for introductions.

References

Abbott, A. and Barman, E. (1997) 'Sequence comparison via alignment and Gibbs sampling: A formal analysis of the emergence of the modern sociological article', *Sociological Methodology*, 27, 47–87.

Abbott, A. and Hrycak, A. (1990) 'Measuring resemblance in sequence data: An optimal matching analysis of musicians' careers', *American Journal of Sociology*, 96, 144–85.

Allison, P.D. (1982) 'Discrete-time Methods for the Analysis of Event Histories', in S. Leinhardt (ed.), *Sociological Methodology 1982*. San Francisco: Jossey-Bass. pp. 61–98.

Allison, P.D. (1984) *Event History Analysis: Regression for the Social Sciences*. Beverly Hills: Sage.

Allison, P.D. (1990) 'Change scores as dependent variables in regression analysis', in C.C. Clogg (ed.), *Sociological Methodology 1990*. Oxford: Basil Blackwell. pp. 93–114.

American Statistical Association (1974) 'The Report of the ASA Conference on Surveys on Human Populations', *American Statistician*, 28, 30–104.

Andress, H.J. (1989) 'Unobserved Heterogeneity in Rate Models: Does It Matter? A Monte-Carlo Study of Different Rate Models Using Generalised Linear Models', *Methodika*, 3, 1–24.

Baltes, P.B. and Nesselroade, J.R. (1973) 'The developmental analysis of individual differences on multiple measures', in J.R. Nesselroade and H.W. Reese (eds), *Life-Span Developmental Psychology: Methodological Issues*. New York: Academic Press.

Baltes, P.B. and Nesselroade, J.R. (1979) 'History and rationale of longitudinal research', in J.R. Nesselroade and P.B. Baltes (eds), *Longitudinal Research in the Study of Behavior and Development*. New York: Academic Press. pp. 1–39.

Baumrind, D. (1983) 'Specious causal attributions in the social sciences', *Journal of Personality and Social Psychology*, 45, 1289–98.

Becker, G.S. (1981) *Treatise on the Family*. Cambridge, MA: Cambridge University Press.

Becker, H.A. (1993) 'A pattern of generations and its consequences', in H.A. Becker (ed.), *Dynamics of Cohort and Generations Research*. Amsterdam: Thesis Publishers. pp. 219–48.

Bentler, P.M. (1990) 'Comparative fit indexes in structural models', *Psychological Bulletin*, 107, 238–46.

Bentler, P.M. and Bonett, D.G. (1980) 'Significance tests and goodness of fit in the analysis of covariance structures', *Psychological Bulletin*, 88, 588–606.

Berger, P. and Luckman, T. (1966) *The Social Construction of Reality: A Treatise in the Sociology of Knowledge*. New York: Anchor Books.

Bernard, H.R., Killworth, P., Kronenfeld, D. and Sailer, L. (1984) 'The problem of informant accuracy: The validity of retrospective data', *Annual Review of Anthropology*, 13, 495–517.

Blalock, H.M. (1962) 'Four-variable causal models and partial correlations', *American Journal of Sociology*, 68, 182–94.

Blalock, H.M. (1964) *Causal Inference in Nonexperimental Research*. New York: Norton.

Blossfeld, H.P. (1993) 'Birth cohorts and their opportunities in the Federal Republic of Germany', in H.A. Becker (ed.), *Dynamics of Cohort and Generations Research*. Amsterdam: Thesis Publishers. pp. 97–138.

Blossfeld, H.P. and Röhwer, G. (1995) *Techniques of Event History Modeling: New Approaches to Causal Analysis*. Mahwah, NJ: Lawrence Erlbaum.

Blossfeld, H.P. and Röhwer, G. (1997) 'Causal inference, time and observation plans in the social sciences', *Quality & Quantity*, 31, 361–84.

Blossfeld, H.P., Hamerle, A. and Mayer, K.U. (1989) *Event History Analysis: Statistical Theory and Application in the Social Sciences*. New Jersey: Lawrence Erlbaum.

Bollen, K.A. (1989) *Structural Equations with Latent Variables*. New York: Wiley.

Boyle, F.M., Najman, J.M., Vance, J.C. and Thearle, M.J. (1996) 'Estimating non-participation bias in a longitudinal study of bereavement', *Australian and New Zealand Journal of Public Health*, 20, 483–7.

Bray, J.H. and Maxwell, S.E. (1985) *Multivariate Analysis of Variance*. Beverly Hills, CA: Sage.

British Psychological Society (1991) *Code of Conduct, Ethical Principles and Guidelines*. Leicester: BPS.

Burchell, B. and Marsh, C. (1992) 'The effect of questionnaire length on survey response', *Quality & Quantity*, 26, 233–44.

Burr, J.A. and Nesselroade, J.R. (1990) 'Change measurement', in A. von Eye (ed.), *Statistical Methods in Longitudinal Research*. Boston: Academic Press. pp. 3–34.

Campbell, D.T. and Stanley, J.C. (1963) *Experimental and Quasi-experimental Designs for Research*. Chicago: Rand McNally.

Campbell, R.T. (1988) 'Integrating conceptualization, design, and analysis in panel studies of the life course', in K.W. Schaie, R.T. Campbell, W. Meredith and S.C. Rawlings (eds), *Methodological Issues in Aging Research*. New York: Springer. pp. 43–69.

Catania, J.A., McDermott, L.J. and Pollack, L.M. (1986) 'Questionnaire response bias and face-to-face interview sample bias in sexuality research', *Journal of Sex Research*, 22, 52–72.

Church, A.H. (1993) 'Estimating the effect of incentives on mail survey response rates: A meta-analysis', *Public Opinion Quarterly*, 57, 62–79.

Claes, R., Quintanilla, A.R. and Whitely, W. (1992) 'Career preparation patterns', *Revue Internationale du Psychologie Sociale*, 5, 37–60.

Cook, T.D. and Campbell, D.T. (1979) *Quasi-experimentation: Design and Analysis Issues for Field Settings*. Boston, MA: Houghton Mifflin.

Costa, P.T. and McCrae, R.R. (1982) 'An approach to the attribution of aging, period and cohort effects', *Psychological Bulletin*, 92, 238–50.

Cox, R.D. (1972) 'Regression models and life tables', *Journal of the Royal Statistical Society series B*, 34, 187–220.

Cox, R.D. (1975) 'Partial likelihood', *Biometrika*, 62, 269–76.

Cox, R.D. and Oakes, D. (1984) *Analysis of Survival Data*. London: Chapman and Hall.

Cronbach, L.J. (1984) *Essentials of Psychological Testing* (4th edn). New York: Harper and Row.

Cronbach, L.J. and Furby, L. (1970) 'How we should measure change – Or should we?', *Psychological Bulletin*, 74, 32–49.

Crowder, M.J. and Hand, D.J. (1990) *Analysis of Repeated Measures*. London: Chapman and Hall.

De Jong-Gierveld, J. (1987) 'Developing and testing a model of loneliness', *Journal of Personality and Social Psychology*, 53, 119–28.

De Jong-Gierveld, J. and Kamphuis, F. (1985) 'The development of a Rasch-type loneliness scale', *Applied Psychological Measurement*, 9, 289–99.

Deville, J.C. and Saporta, G. (1983) 'Correspondence analysis, with an extension towards nominal time series', *Journal of Econometrics*, 22, 169–89.

Diekmann, A., Jungbauer-Gans, M., Krassnig, H. and Lorenz, S. (1996) 'Social status and aggression: A field study analyzed by survival analysis', *Journal of Social Psychology*, 136, 761–8.

Diggle, P. and Kenward, M.G. (1994) 'Informative drop-out in longitudinal data analysis', *Applied Statistics*, 43, 49–94.

Dijkstra, W.D. and Smit, J. (1993) 'Nonrespons' (non-response), in W. Dijkstra (ed.), *Het Proces van Sociale Intergratie van Jong-volwassenen*. Amsterdam: Vrije Universiteit. pp. 59–70.

Dijkstra, W.D. and Taris, T.W. (1995) 'Measuring the agreement between sequences', *Sociological Methods and Research*, 24, 214–31.

Dillman, D.A. (1978) *Mail and Telephone Surveys: The Total Design Method*. New York: Wiley.

Doolittle, R.F. (ed.) (1990) *Methods in Enzymology*, vol. 183: *Molecular Evolution: Computer Analysis of Protein and Nucleic and Acid Sequences*. New York: Academic Press.

Eaker, S., Bergström, R., Bergström, A., Adami, H.O. and Nyren, O. (1998) 'Response rate to mailed epidemiologic questionnaires: A population-based randomized trial of variations in design and mailing routines', *American Journal of Epidemiology*, 147, 74–82.

Elandt-Johnson, R.C. and Johnson, N.L. (1980) *Survival Models and Data Analysis*. New York: Wiley.

Ellickson, P.L., Bianca, D. and Schoeff, D.C. (1988) 'Containing attrition in school-based research: An innovative approach', *Evaluation Review*, 12, 331–51.

Ellish, N.J., Weisman, C.S., Celentano, D. and Zenilman, J.M. (1996) 'Reliability of partner reports of sexual history in a heterosexual population at a sexually transmitted diseases clinic', *Sexually Transmitted Diseases*, 23, 446–52.

Emmerich, W. (1968) 'Personality development and concepts of structure', *Child Development*, 39, 671–90.

Engel, E. (1857) 'Die Produktions- und Konsumptionsverhältnisse des Königreichs Sachsen', Zeitschrift des Statistischen Büreaus des Könlich Sachsischen Ministerium des Inneren, 22 November 1857. In E. Engel (1885), Die Lebenskosten Belgischer Arbeiterfamilien früher und jetzt (Appendix E). *Bulletin de l'Institut International de Statistique*, 9, 1–24.

Engel, U. and Reinecke, J. (1994) *Panelanalyse: Grundlagen, Techniken, Beispiele.* Berlin: Walter de Gruyter.

Everitt, B. (1981) *Cluster Analysis.* Beverly Hills, CA: Sage.

Feij, J.A., Peiro, J.M., Whitely, W.T. and Taris, T.W. (1995), 'The development of career enhancing strategies, and content innovation: A longitudinal study of new workers', *Journal of Vocational Behavior*, 46, 231–56.

Finn, J.D. (1974) *A General Model for Multivariate Analysis.* New York: Holt, Rinehart and Winston.

Freedman, D., Thornton, A., Camburn, D., Alwin, D. and Young-DeMarco, L. (1988) 'The life history calendar: A technique for collecting retrospective data', in C.C. Clogg (ed.), *Sociological Methodology*, vol. 18. San Francisco: Jossey-Bass. pp. 37–68.

Freedman, D.P., Gallagher, B., Morley, L., Ledger, R.J. and West, D.J. (1990) 'Minimizing attrition in longitudinal research: Methods of tracing and securing cooperation in a 24-year follow-up study', in D. Magnusson and L.R. Bergman (eds), *Data Quality in Longitudinal Research.* Cambridge: Cambridge University Press. pp. 122–47.

Freeman, R.A. (1991) 'Statistical analysis and shoe leather', *Sociological Methodology*, 21, 291–313.

Furby, L. (1973) 'Interpreting regression toward the mean in development research', *Developmental Psychology*, 8, 172–9.

Gergen, K.J. (1977) 'Stability, change, and chance in understanding human development', in N. Datan and H.W. Reese (eds), *Life-Span Developmental Psychology: Dialectical Perspectives on Experimental Research.* New York: Academic Press.

Gifi, A. (1990) *Nonlinear Multivariate Analysis.* New York: Wiley.

Glenn, N.D. (1981) 'The utility and logic of cohort analysis', *Journal of Applied Behavioral Science*, 17, 247–57.

Glenn, N.D. and McLanahan, S. (1982), 'Children and marital happiness: A further specification of the relationship', *Journal of Marriage and the Family*, 44, 63–72.

Gmel, G. (1996), 'Response behavior to questions on alcohol consumption: Non-response bias in mailed follow-up questionnaires', *Schweizerische Zeitschrift für Soziologie*, 22, 285–301.

Goldberg, D. (1972) *The Detection of Psychiatric Illness by Questionnaire.* London: Oxford University Press.

Goldman, N., Vaughan, B. and Pebley, A.R. (1998) 'The use of calendars to measure child illness in health interview surveys', *International Journal of Epidemiology*, 27, 505–12.

Golembiewski, R.T., Billingsley, K. and Yeager, S. (1976) 'Measuring change and persistency in human affairs: Types of change generated by OD designs', *Journal of Applied Behavioural Science*, 12, 133–57.

Goodman, J.S. and Blum, T.C. (1996) 'Assessing the non-random sampling effects of subject attrition in longitudinal research', *Journal of Management*, 22, 627–52.

Gould, S.J. (1991) *Bully for Brontosaurus: Further Reflections in Natural History.* London: Penguin.

Goyder, J. (1987) *The Silent Minority.* Cambridge: Cambridge University Press.

Greenacre, M.J. (1984) *Theory and Applications of Correspondence Analysis.* New York: Academic Press.

Griffin, L.J. (1992) 'Temporality, events, and explanation in historical sociology', *Sociological Methods & Research*, 20, 403–27.

Grimsmo, A., Helgesen, G. and Borchgrevink, C. (1981) 'Short-term and long-term effects of lay groups on weight reduction', *British Medical Journal*, 283, 1093–5.

Groenland, E.A.G. and Van de Stadt, H. (1985) 'Sociaal Economisch Panelonderzoek onder Huishoudens' (Socio-economic research among households), *CBS-Select*, 3, 89–103.

Hachen, D.S. (1988) 'The competing risks model: A method for analyzing processes with multiple types of events', *Sociological Methods and Research*, 17, 21–54.

Hand, D. and Crowder, M. (1996) *Practical Longitudinal Data Analysis*. London: Chapman and Hall.

Hand, D.J. and Taylor, C.C. (1987) *Multivariate Analysis of Variance and Repeated Measures: A Practical Approach for Behavioral Scientists*. London: Chapman and Hall.

Hayduk, L.A. (1989) *Structural Modelling with LISREL: Essentials and Advances*. Baltimore: Johns Hopkins University Press.

Heckman, J. and Singer, B. (1984) 'A method for minimizing the impact of distributional assumptions in economietric models for duration data', *Econometrica*, 52, 271–320.

Helwig, A.A. and Myrin, M.D. (1997) 'Ten-year stability of Holland codes within one family', *Career Development Quarterly*, 46, 62–71.

Hogan, D.P. (1978) 'The variable order of events in the life course', *American Sociological Review*, 45, 573–86.

Hox, J.J. and De Leeuw, E.D. (1994) 'A comparison of nonresponse in mail, telephone, and face-to-face surveys: Applying multilevel modeling to meta-analysis', *Quality & Quantity*, 28, 329–44.

Hox, J., De Leeuw, E. and Vorst, H. (1995) 'Survey participation as reasoned action: A behavioral paradigm for survey nonresponse?', *Bulletin de Méthodologie Sociologique*, 48, 52–67.

Hsiao, C. (1986) *Analysis of Panel Data*. Cambridge: Cambridge University Press.

Hsu, L.M. (1995) 'Regression toward the mean associatied with measurement error and the identification of improvement and deterioration in psychotherapy', *Journal of Consulting and Clinical Psychology*, 63, 141–4.

Hubert, L.J. (1979) 'Comparison of sequences', *Psychological Bulletin*, 86, 1098–106.

Hutchison, D. (1988a) 'Event history and survival analysis in the social sciences I: Background and introduction', *Quality & Quantity*, 22, 203–19.

Hutchison, D. (1988b) 'Event history and survival analysis in the social sciences II: Advanced applications and recent developments', *Quality & Quantity*, 22, 255–78.

Ito, P.K. (1980) 'Robustness of ANOVA and MANOVA test procedures', in P.R. Krishnaiah (ed.), *Handbook of Statistics*, vol. I: *Analysis of Variance*. Amsterdam: North-Holland. pp. 199–236.

Iversen, G.R. and Norpoth, H. (1982) *Analysis of Variance*. Beverly Hills, CA: Sage.

Jennings, M.K. and Markus, G.B. (1977) 'The effects of military service on political attitude: A panel study', *American Political Science Review*, 71, 131–47.

Johanson, E. (1987) 'Registration of longitudinal data by means of musical notation', *Quality & Quantity*, 21, 59–69.

Johanson, E. (1991) 'High-precision registration of complicated longitudinal and cross-sectional data', *Quality & Quantity*, 25, 321–6.

Jöreskog, K.G. (1967) 'Some contributions to maximum likelihood factor analysis', *Psychometrika*, 34, 183–202.

Jöreskog, K.G. (1969) 'A general approach to confirmatory factor analysis', *Psychometrika*, 36, 409–26.

Jöreskog, K.G. (1979a) 'Longitudinal covariance structure models', in K.G. Jöreskog and D. Sörbom (eds), *Advances in Factor Analysis and Structural Equation Models*. Cambridge, MA: Abt Books.

Jöreskog, K.G. (1979b) 'Basic ideas of factor and component analysis', in K.G. Jöreskog and D. Sörbom (eds), *Advances in Factor Analysis and Structural Equation Models*. Cambridge, MA: Abt Books.

Jöreskog, K.G. and Sörbom, D. (1993) *LISREL-8* (computer manual) Chicago: Scientific Software.

Kagan, J. (1980) 'Perspectives on continuity', in O.J. Brim and J. Kagan (eds), *Constancy and Change in Human Development*. Cambridge, MA: Harvard University Press.

Kalton, G. and Kasprzyk, D. (1986) 'The treatment of missing data', *Survey Methodology*, 12, 1–16.

Karweit, N. and Kertzer, D.I. (1986) 'Data base management for life course family research', *Current Perspectives on Aging and the Life Cycle*, 2, 167–88.

Kenny, D.A. (1975) 'Cross-lagged panel correlation: A test for spuriousness', *Psychological Bulletin*, 82, 887–903.

Kenny, D.A. and Cohen, S.H. (1979) 'A reexamination of selection and growth processes in the nonequivalent control group design', in K.F. Schuessler (ed.), *Sociological Methodology 1980*. San Francisco: Jossey-Bass. pp. 290–313.

Kenny, D.A. and Harackiewicz, J.M. (1979) 'Cross-lagged panel correlation: Practice and promise', *Journal of Applied Psychology*, 64, 372–9.

Kenward, M.G. (1987) 'A method for comparing profiles of repeated measurements', *Applied Statistics*, 36, 296–308.

Kessler, R.C. (1977) 'Use of change scores as criteria in longitudinal survey research', *Quality & Quantity*, 11, 43–66.

Kessler, R.C. and Greenberg, D.F. (1981) *Linear Panel Analysis: Models of Quantitative Change*. New York: Academic Press.

Kessler, R.C., Little, R.J.A. and Groves, R.M. (1995) 'Advances in strategies for minimizing and adjusting for survey nonresponse', *Epidemiologic Reviews*, 17, 192–204.

Kim, J.O. and Mueller, C.W. (1978a) *Introduction to Factor Analysis: What It Is, and How to Do It*. Beverly Hills, CA: Sage.

Kim, J.O. and Mueller, C.W. (1978b) *Factor Analysis*. Beverly Hills, CA: Sage.

Kreiger, N. and Nishri, E.D. (1997) 'The effect of nonresponse on estimation of relative risk in a case-control study', *Annals of Epidemiology*, 7, 194–9.

Lazarsfeld, P.F. (1946/1972) 'Mutual effects of statistical variables', in P.F. Lazarsfeld, A.K. Pasanella and M. Rosenberg (eds), *Continuities in the Language of Social Research*. New York: The Free Press. pp. 388–98.

Lazarsfeld, P.F. and Fiske, M. (1938) 'The panel as a new tool for measuring opinion', *Public Opinion Quarterly*, 2, 596–612.

Linton, M. (1982) 'Transformations of memory in everyday life', in U. Neisser (ed.), *Memory Observed: Remembering in Natural Contexts*. New York: Freeman & Company. pp. 78–91.

Little, R.J.A. (1995). 'Modeling the drop-out mechanism in repeated-measures studies', *Journal of the American Statistical Association*, 90, 1112–21.

Little, R.J.A. and Rubin, D.B. (1987) *Statistical Analysis with Missing Data*. New York: John Wiley.

Little, R.J.A. and Rubin, D.B. (1990) 'The analysis of social science data with missing values', *Sociological Methods and Research*, 18, 292–326.

Loehlin, J.C. (1998) *Latent Variable Models: An Introduction to Factor, Path, and Structural Analysis* (3rd edn). Mahwah, NJ: Lawrence Erlbaum.

Loftus, E.F. and Marburger, W. (1983) 'Since the eruption of Mnt. St. Helens, has anyone beaten you up? Improving the accuracy of retrospective reports with landmark events', *Memory and Cognition*, 11, 114–20.

Long, J.S. (1983a) *Confirmatory Factor Analysis*. Beverly Hills, CA: Sage.

Long, J.S. (1983b) *Covariance Structure Models: An Introduction to LISREL*. Beverly Hills, CA: Sage.

Long, J.S., Allison, P.D. and McGinnis, R. (1979) 'Entrance into the academic career', *American Sociological Review*, 44, 816–30.

Lord, F.M. (1963) 'Elementary models for measuring change', in W.C. Harris (ed.), *Problems in Measuring Change*. Madison: University of Wisconsin Press. pp. 21–38.

Lund, E. and Gram, I.T. (1998) 'Response rate according to title and length of questionnaire', *Scandinavian Journal of Social Medicine*, 26, 154–60.

MacCallum, R.C., Roznowski, M. and Necowitz, L.B. (1992) 'Model modifications in covariance structure analysis: The problem of capitalization on chance', *Psychological Bulletin*, 111, 490–504.

Mannheim, K. (1928/1929) 'Das Problem der Generationen', *Kölner Vierteljahreshefte für Soziologie*, 7, 157–89 and 309–30.

Marini, M.M. and Singer, B. (1988) 'Causality in the social sciences', in C.C. Clogg (ed.), *Sociological Methodology 18*. San Francisco: Jossey-Bass. pp. 347–409.

Markus, G.B. (1979) *Analyzing Panel Data*. Beverly Hills, CA: Sage.

Martin, C.L. (1994) 'The impact of topic interest on mail survey response behaviour', *Journal of the Market Research Society*, 36, 327–38.

Maslach, C. and Jackson, S.E. (1986) *MBI: Maslach Burnout Inventory*. Palo Alto, CA: Consulting Psychologists Press, Inc.

Mason, K.O., Mason, W.M., Winsborough, H.H. and Poole, W.K. (1973) 'Some methodological issues in cohort analysis of archival data', *American Sociological Review*, 38, 242–58.

Maxwell, S.W. and Howard, G.S. (1981) 'Change scores: Necessarily an anathema?', *Educational and Psychological Meaurement*, 41, 747–56.

Maynard, M.L. (1996) 'Effectiveness of begging as a persuasive tactic for improving response rate on a client agency mail survey', *Psychological Reports*, 78, 204–6.

McArdle, J.J. and Aber, M.S. (1990) 'Patterns of change within latent variable structural equation models', in A. von Eye (ed.), *Statistical Methods in Longitudinal Research*, vol. I. Boston: Academic Press.

McBride, T.D., Calsyn, R.J., Morse, G.A., Klinkenberg, W.D. and Allen, G.A. (1998) 'Duration of homeless spells among severely mentally ill individuals: A survival analysis', *Journal of Community Psychology*, 26, 473–90.

McGinnis, R. (1968) 'A stochastic model of social mobility', *American Sociological Review*, 33 (5), 712–21.

Menard, S. (1991) *Longitudinal Research*. Beverly Hills, CA: Sage.

Mihelic, A.H. and Crimmins, E.M. (1997) 'Loss to follow-up in a sample of Americans 70 years of age and older: The LSOA 1984–1990', *Journals of Gerontology, Series B – Psychological Sciences and Social Sciences*, 52, S37–S48.

Millsap, R.E. (1991) 'Confirmatory measurement models model comparisons using latent means', *Multivariate Behavioral Research*, 26, 479–97.

Millsap, R.E. and Hartog, S.B. (1988) 'Alpha, beta, and gamma change in evaluation research: A structural equation approach', *Journal of Applied Psychology*, 73, 574–84.

Mortimer, J.D., Finch, M.D. and Kumka, D. (1982) 'Persistence and change in development: The multidimensional self-concept', in P.B. Baltes and O.G Brim (eds), *Life-Span Development and Behavior*, vol. 4. New York: Academic Press. pp. 263–309.

Nederhof, A.J. (1988) 'Effects of a final telephone reminder and questionnaire cover design in mail surveys', *Social Science Research*, 17, 353–61.

Nesselroade, J.R. and Baltes, P.B. (1979) *Longitudinal Research in the Study of Behavior and Development*. New York: Academic Press.

Nicholson, N. (1987) 'Work-role transitions: Processes and outcomes', in P.B. Warr (ed.), *Psychology at Work*. Harmondsworth: Penguin. pp. 160–77.

Nordström, P., Samuelsson, M. and Asberg, M. (1995) 'Survival analysis of suicide risk after attempted suicide', *Acta Psychiatrica Scandinavica*, 91, 336–40.

Parmar, M.K.B. and Machin, D. (1995) *Survival Analysis: A Practical Approach*. New York: Wiley.

Patterson, G.R. (1993) 'Orderly change in a stable world: The antisocial trait as a chimera', *Journal of Consulting and Clinical Psychology*, 61, 911–19.

Pentz, M.A. and Chou, C.P. (1994) 'Measurement invariance in longitudinal clinical research assuming change from development and intervention', *Journal of Consulting and Clinical Psychology*, 62, 450–62.

Petersen, T. (1986) 'Estimating fully parametric hazard rate models with time-dependent covariates: Use of maximum likelihood', *Sociological Methods & Research*, 14, 219–46.

Plewis, I. (1985) *Analysing Change: Measurement and Explanation using Longitudinal Data*. Chichester: Wiley.

Pollard, A.H., Yusuf, F. and Pollard, G.N. (1981) *Demographic Techniques* (2nd edn). Sydney: Pergamon.

Powers, E.A., Goudy, W.J. and Keith, P.M. (1978) 'Congruence between panel and recall data in longitudinal research', *Public Opinion Quarterly*, 42, 380–9.

Raffalovich, L.L. and Knoke, D. (1983) 'Quantitative methods for the analysis of historical change', *Historical Methods*, 16, 149–54.

Rao, D.N., Shroff, P.D., Chattopadhyay, G. and Dinshaw, K.A. (1998) 'Survival analysis of 5595 head and neck cancers: Results of conventional treatment in a high-risk population', *British Journal of Cancer*, 77, 1514–18.

Robson, C. (1993) *Real World Research: A Resource for Social Scientists and Practitioner-Researchers*. Oxford: Blackwell.

Rodgers, W.L. (1982) 'Estimable functions of age, period, and cohort effects', *American Sociological Review*, 47, 774–87.

Rogosa, D. (1988) 'Myths about longitudinal research', in K.W. Schaie, R.T.

Campbell, W. Meredith and S.C. Rawlings (eds), *Methodological Issues in Aging Research*. New York: Springer. pp. 171–209.

Rogosa, D.R. and Willett, J.B. (1985) 'Understanding correlates of change by modeling individual differences in growth', *Psychometrika*, 50, 203–28.

Rosenbaum, J.E. (1979) 'Tournament mobility: Career patterns in a corporation', *Administrative Science Quarterly*, 24, 220–41.

Rovine, M.J. and Von Eye, A. (1991) *Applied Computational Statistics in Longitudinal Research*. Boston: Academic Press.

Ryder, N.B. (1965) 'The cohort as a concept in the study of social change', *American Sociological Review*, 30, 843–61.

Sandefur, G.D. and Tuma, N.B. (1987) 'How data type affects conclusions about individual mobility', *Social Science Research*, 16, 301–28.

Saporta, G. (1981) *Méthodes Exploratoires d'Analyse de Données Temporelles* (unpublished doctoral dissertation). Paris: Université P. et M. Curie.

Saris, W. (1991) *Computer-Assisted Interviewing*. Beverly Hills, CA: Sage.

Schaie, K.W. (1965) 'A general model for the study of developmental problems', *Psychological Bulletin*, 64, 92–107.

Schaie, K.W. and Herzog, C. (1982) 'Longitudinal methods', in B.B. Wolman (ed.), *Handbook of Developmental Psychology*. Englewood Cliffs, NJ: Prentice-Hall. pp. 351–86.

Schaie, K.W., Willis, S.L., Jay, G. and Chipuer, H. (1989) 'Structural invariance of cognitive abilities across the adult life span: A cross-sectional study', *Developmental Psychology*, 24, 652–62.

Schaubroeck, J. and Green, S.G. (1989) 'Confirmatory factor analytic procedures for assessing change during organizational entry', *Journal of Applied Psychology*, 74, 892–900.

Schmitt, N. (1982) 'The use of analysis of covariance structures to assess beta and gamma change', *Multivariate Behavioral Research*, 17, 343–58.

Schmitt, N., Pulakos, E.D. and Lieblein, A. (1984) 'Comparison of three techniques to assess group-level beta and gamma change', *Applied Psychological Measurement*, 8, 249–60.

Schwarz, N. (1990) 'Assessing frequency reports of mundane behaviors: Contributions of cognitive psychology to questionnaire construction', in C. Hendrick and M.S. Clark (eds), *Review of Personality and Social Psychology*, vol. 11: *Research Methods in Personality and Social Psychology*. Beverly Hills, CA: Sage. pp. 98–119.

Schwarz, N. (1996) 'Survey research: Collecting data by asking questions', in G.R. Semin and K. Fiedler (eds), *Applied Social Psychology*. London: Sage. pp. 65–90.

Schwarz, N. and Sudman, S. (eds) (1994) *Autobiographical Memory and the Validity of Retrospective Reports*. New York: Springer Verlag.

Schweitzer, M. and Asch, D.A. (1995) 'Timing payments to subjects of mail surveys: Cost-effectiveness and bias', *Journal of Clinical Epidemiology*, 48, 1325–9.

Sharma, K.K. and Gupta, J.K. (1986) 'Optimum reliability of gain scores', *Journal of Experimental Education*, 54, 105–8.

Shingles, R.D. (1985) 'Causal inference in cross-lagged panel analysis', in H.M. Blalock (ed.), *Causal Models in Panel and Experimental Designs*. New York: Aldine. pp. 219–49.

Singer, E., Von Thurn, D.R. and Miller, E.R. (1995) 'Confidentiality assurances and response: A quantitative review of the experimental literature', *Public Opinion Quarterly*, 59, 66–77.

Smith, T.W. (1995) 'Trends in non-response rates', *International Journal of Public Opinion Research*, 7, 157–71.

Sontag, L.W. (1971) 'The history of longitudinal research: Implications for the future', *Child Development*, 42, 987–1002.

Speer, D.C. (1992) 'Clinically significant change: Jacobson and Truax (1991) revisited', *Journal of Consulting and Clinical Psychology*, 60, 402–8.

Spencer, T.F. and McCall, R. (1982) *Career Development of American Managers*. New York: Academic Press.

Steeh, C.G. (1981) 'Trends in nonresponse rates, 1952–1979', *Public Opinion Quarterly*, 45, 40–57.

Stroebe, W. and Stroebe, M.S. (1993) 'Determinants of adjustment to bereavement in younger widows and widowers', in M.S. Stroebe and W. Stroebe (eds), *Handbook of Bereavement: Theory, Research, and Intervention*. New York: Cambridge University Press. pp. 208–26.

Taris, T.W. (1996) 'Modeling nonresponse in multiwave panel studies using discrete-time Markov models', *Quality & Quantity*, 30, 189–203.

Taris, T.W. (1997) 'On selectivity of nonresponse in discrete-time multi-wave panel studies', *Quality & Quantity*, 31, 79–94.

Taris, T.W. and Bok, I.A. (1998) 'On gender specificity of person characteristics in personnel advertisements: A study among future applicants', *The Journal of Social Psychology*, 132, 593–610.

Taris, T.W., Bok, I.A. and Caljé, D.G. (1998) 'On the relation among job characteristics and depression: Evidence for reciprocal effects?', *International Journal of Stress Management*, 5, 157–67.

Taris, T.W., Bok, I.A. and Meijer, Z.Y. (1998) 'On assessing stability and change of psychometric properties of multi-item concepts across different situations: Three applications of an eight-step procedure', *Journal of Psychology*, 132, 301–27.

Taris, T.W. and Feij, J.A. (1997) 'Shifts in the educational and vocational careers of Dutch young adults during the eighties: On the decreasing pay-off of education', *International Journal of Adolescence and Youth*, 6, 273–94.

Taris, T.W. and Feij, J.A. (1999) 'Measuring career mobility: An empirical comparison of six mobility indexes', *Quality & Quantity*, 33, 157–68.

Taris, T.W., Schreurs, P.J.G., and Schaufeli, W.B. (2000) 'Construct validity of the Maslach Burnout Inventory – General Survey: A two-sample examination of its factor structure and correlates'. *Work & Stress*, 13, 223–37.

Taris, T.W. and Semin, G.R. (1995) 'Does adolescents' sexual behaviour affect their attitudes concerning sex?', *International Journal of Adolescence and Youth*, 5, 139–56.

Taris, T.W. and Semin, G.R. (1997) 'Gender as a moderator of the effects of the love motive and relational context on sexual experience', *Archives of Sexual Behavior*, 26, 159–80.

Taris, T.W., Semin, G.R. and Bok, I.A. (1998) 'Quality of family interaction and intergenerational transmission of values: The case of sexual permissiveness', *Journal of Genetic Psychology*, 159, 237–50.

Taylor, J. and Cuave, K.L. (1995) 'The sophomore slump among professional baseball players: Real or imagined?', *International Journal of Sport Psychology*, 25, 230–9.

Thorndike, E.L. (1924) 'The influence of chance imperfections of measures upon the relationship of initial score to gain or loss', *Journal of Experimental Psychology*, 7, 225–32.

Thornton, A., Freedman, D.S. and Camburn, D. (1982) 'Obtaining respondent cooperation in family panel studies', *Sociological Methods & Research*, 11, 33–51.

Trussell, J. and Richards, T. (1985) 'Correcting for unmeasured heterogeneity in hazard models using the Heckman-Singer Procedure', in N.B. Tuma (ed.), *Sociological Methodology 1985*. San Francisco: Jossey-Bass. pp. 242–76.

Tuma, N.B. and Hannan, M.T. (1984) *Social Dynamics: Models and Methods*. New York: Lawrence Erlbaum.

Van de Pol, F.J.R. (1989) *Issues of Design and Analysis of Panels*. Amsterdam: Sociometric Research Foundation.

Van der Heijden, P.G.M. and De Leeuw, J. (1989) 'Correspondence analysis, with special attention to the analysis of panel data and event histories', *Sociological Methodology 1989*. Oxford: Basil Blackwell. pp. 43–87.

Van der Heijden, P.G.M., Teunissen, J. and Van Orle, C. (1997) 'Multiple correspondence analysis as a tool for quantification or classification of career data', *Journal of Educational and Behavioral Statistics*, 22, 447–77.

Van der Vaart, W. (1996) *Inquiring into the Past: Data Quality of Responses to Retrospective Questions*. Amsterdam: Free University Amsterdam (unpublished Ph.D.-thesis).

Vermunt, J.K. (1997) *Log-linear Models for Event Histories*. Thousand Oaks, CA: Sage.

Waite, L.J. and Stolzenberg, R.M. (1976) 'Intended childbearing and labor force participation of young women: Insights from nonrecursive models', *American Sociological Review*, 41, 235–51.

Waterton, J. and Lievesley, D. (1987) 'Attrition in a panel study of attitudes', *Journal of Official Statistics*, 3, 267–82.

Werts, C.E. and Linn, R.L. (1970) 'A general linear model for studying growth', *Psychological Bulletin*, 73, 17–22.

Wilder, J. (1967) *Stimulus and Response: The Law of Initial Value*. Bristol: Wright.

Willekens, F.J. (1991) 'Understanding the interdependence between parallel careers', in J.J. Siegers, J. de Jong-Gierveld and E. van Imhoff (eds), *Female Labour Market Behaviour and Fertility: A Rational-choice Approach*. Berlin: Springer Verlag. pp. 2–31.

Winer, B.J. (1971) *Statistical Principles in Experimental Design*. Tokyo: McGraw-Hill Kogakusha.

Winkler, R.L. and Hays, W.L. (1971) *Statistics: Probability, Inference, and Decision*. New York: Holt, Rinehart and Winston.

WOSY International Research Group (1989) 'Socializacion laboral del joven: Un estudio transnacional' (Work socialization of youth: A cross-national study), *Papeles del Psicologico*, issue 38.

Yamaguchi, K. (1991) *Event History Analysis*. Newbury Park, CA: Sage.

Zuckerman, M. (1994) *Behavioral Expressions and Biosocial Bases of Sensation Seeking*. Cambridge: Cambridge University Press.

Author Index

Subject index